# First Corinthians

INTERPRETATION
BIBLE STUDIES

Other Interpretation Bible Studies
from Westminster John Knox Press

*Genesis*
Celia Brewer Marshall

*Exodus*
James D. Newsome

*First and Second Samuel*
David Hester

*Esther and Ruth*
Patricia K. Tull

*Psalms*
Jerome F. D. Creach

*Isaiah*
Gary W. Light

*Jeremiah*
Robert R. Laha Jr.

*Matthew*
Alyce M. McKenzie

*Mark*
Richard I. Deibert

*Luke*
Thomas W. Walker

*John*
Mark A. Matson

*Acts*
Charles C. Williamson

*Romans*
Art Ross and Martha M. Stevenson

*First Corinthians*
Bruce N. Fisk

*Second Corinthians*
William M. Ramsay

*Philippians and Galatians*
Stanley P. Saunders

*Revelation*
William C. Pender

# First Corinthians

BRUCE N. FISK

Westminster John Knox Press
LOUISVILLE • LONDON

Unless otherwise noted, scripture translations are those of the author.



Grateful acknowledgment is made to Bethany House for permission to reproduce "The In's and Out's of It," by John Fischer, from his book *Real Christians Don't Dance* (Minneapolis: Bethany House, 1988).



*Book design by Drew Stevens*
*Cover design by Pam Poll*
*Cover illustration by Robert Stratton*

*First edition*
Published by Westminster John Knox Press
Louisville, Kentucky

This book is printed on acid-free paper that meets the American National Standards Institute Z39.48 standard. ♾

PRINTED IN THE UNITED STATES OF AMERICA

06 07 08 09 — 10 9 8 7 6 5 4

**Library of Congress Cataloging-in-Publication Data**

A catalog record for this book is available from the Library of Congress.

ISBN-13: 978-0-664-22692-3
ISBN-10: 0-664-22692-2

# Contents

# Series Introduction

The Bible has long been revered for its witness to God's presence and redeeming activity in the world; its message of creation and judgment, love and forgiveness, grace and hope; its memorable characters and stories; its challenges to human life; and its power to shape faith. For generations people have found in the Bible inspiration and instruction, and, for nearly as long, commentators and scholars have assisted students of the Bible. This series, Interpretation Bible Studies (IBS), continues that great heritage of scholarship with a fresh approach to biblical study.

Designed for ease and flexibility of use for either personal or group study, IBS helps readers not only to learn about the history and theology of the Bible, understand the sometimes difficult language of biblical passages, and marvel at the biblical accounts of God's activity in human life, but also to accept the challenge of the Bible's call to discipleship. IBS offers sound guidance for deepening one's knowledge of the Bible and for faithful Christian living in today's world.

IBS was developed out of three primary convictions. First, the Bible is the church's scripture and stands in a unique place of authority in Christian understanding. Second, good scholarship helps readers understand the truths of the Bible and sharpens their perception of God speaking through the Bible. Third, deep knowledge of the Bible bears fruit in one's ethical and spiritual life.

Each IBS volume has ten brief units of key passages from a book of the Bible. By moving through these units, readers capture the sweep of the whole biblical book. Each unit includes study helps, such as maps, photos, definitions of key terms, questions for reflection, and suggestions for resources for further study. In the back of each volume is a Leader's Guide that offers helpful suggestions on how to use IBS.

The Interpretation Bible Studies series grows out of the well-known Interpretation commentaries (John Knox Press), a series that helps preachers and teachers in their preparation. Although each IBS volume bears a deep kinship to its companion Interpretation commentary, IBS can stand alone. The reader need not be familiar with the Interpretation commentary to benefit from IBS. However, those who want to discover even more about the Bible will benefit by consulting Interpretation commentaries too.

Through the kind of encounter with the Bible encouraged by the Interpretation Bible Studies, the church will continue to discover God speaking afresh in the scriptures.

# Introduction to First Corinthians

"First Corinthians has sixteen chapters not, I think, because Saint Paul neatly rounded off his argument at that number but because God, taking pity on subsequent generations of commentators, inspired him at that point to go to bed." So muses Robert Farrar Capon as he ponders the mystery of inspired scripture (Capon, 215). How can an ancient epistle like First Corinthians be so earthy, so homespun, so ad hoc, and yet still find its home within the pages of Sacred Writ? How can private correspondence, filled with uncomplimentary images of a cluster of refractory house churches, qualify for permanent inclusion in the authoritative canon of the New Testament? And how can we, so many years later, expect to glean anything of value for *our* daily struggles simply by reading the mail of a first-century Christian community at a particularly anxious moment in their history?

> "We are literally reading somebody else's mail."—Richard Hays, *First Corinthians*, Interpretation (Louisville, Ky.: John Knox Press, 1997), 1.

Shouldn't the pages of scripture be more reverent? More timeless? More preachy? Why must this portion of the New Testament be preoccupied with petty rivalry (1 Cor. 3:3), deviant sexuality (5:1; 6:15), selfish eating habits (8:10; 11:21), and chaotic church meetings (14:33)? The answer of course is that First Corinthians, like the rest of scripture, was forged and fashioned down here in the real world. This letter is not a detached moral treatise filled with generic platitudes. It does not somehow float along above history, culture, and the real problems of real people. Its author was struggling, as he wrote, to regain the pastoral authority he exercised when the church began

(2:1–5; 4:15). And its first readers, a raucous lot mostly converted out of paganism, suffered from immaturity and all manner of blind spots. Some were rich and snooty; others poor and superstitious; still others proud or judgmental or indifferent.

Fortunately, however, Paul did not hide behind diplomacy or take refuge in subtleties and understatement. His direct responses to the people's shortcomings provide us with a window on the to-and-fro of church life in the first century. But it also paints a vivid picture of what the church, in all its "sweaty, smelly concreteness" (Neuhaus, 10), can become, by the grace of God. First Corinthians is not merely a scandalous exposé that shows where the church so often goes *wrong;* it is also a challenging invitation to the church, to strive together to get it *right.*

We do not know if Paul was optimistic as he sealed up this letter and entrusted it to three members of the Corinthian congregation who would carry it back from Ephesus (16:17–18). But we do know Paul dreamed that they would become, more and more, a Christian community living together in harmony, whose members measured each move in terms of how it edified one another (14:26) or how it advanced the gospel (9:23). We know he yearned to see more love among them of the kind that would finally flourish when Christ returned (13:4–10; 16:14). Most of all, we know he longed to see them return once again to the simple message of the cross in which they first placed their trust.

## Want to Know More?

**About leading Bible study groups?** See Roberta Hestenes, *Using the Bible in Groups* (Philadelphia: Westminster Press, 1983).

**About studying First Corinthians?** See Hays, *First Corinthians,* and William Barclay, *The Letters to the Corinthians,* Daily Study Bible (Philadelphia: Westminster Press, 1975).

**About the city of Corinth?** See Jerome Murphy-O'Connor, *St. Paul's Corinth: Texts and Archaeology* (Wilmington, Del.: Michael Glazier, 1983).

**About Paul's writings?** See Calvin J. Roetzel, *The Letters of Paul: Conversations in Context,* 4th ed. (Louisville, Ky.: Westminster John Knox Press, 1998).

Unfortunately, it is not at all clear that the original recipients of this letter received it as Paul would have liked. Second Corinthians is proof that relations between Paul and the congregation remained strained, and that his apostolic authority remained in dispute. Even four decades later, when Clement, Bishop of Rome, sent another letter their way, the Corinthians church was still noted for its quarrels and divisions. But if Paul lost the battle at Corinth, at least he won the war, for his vision of the church has been shaping the imaginations of Christians ever since. So this set of studies in First Corinthians is simply one more chance for us to reflect together upon the church: as it was, as it is, and as it shall be "when the perfect comes" (13:10).

Those who want to dig deeper would be greatly enriched by two full-length commentaries on First Corinthians. Richard Hays has authored the *First Corinthians* volume in the Interpretation series (John Knox Press, 1997), a work that scores high marks for readability, sound judgment, and practical relevance. The close kinship between Hays's commentary and this study should make it easy for readers to slide back and forth between the two. More technical, but still eminently useful and full of insight, is Gordon Fee's *The First Epistle to the Corinthians* in the New International Commentary series (Eerdmans, 1987).

I dedicate this little volume to the saints who are at Caronport, a small prairie town in western Canada. On those dear friends and colleagues I inflicted several of these studies, and with them I have labored and prayed as we sought to discern what Christ's church should look like "two thousand years and half a world away" from Paul's Corinth. Thanks especially to Chad, Dustin, Bruce, and to my dear wife, Jan, for their thoughtful critique and encouragement as these thoughts took shape.

Biblical citations are from a variety of translations. Below is a list of abbreviations:

| | |
|---|---|
| KJV | King James Version |
| NASV | New American Standard Version |
| NEB | New English Bible |
| NIV | New International Version |
| NJB | New Jerusalem Bible |
| NKJV | New King James Version |
| NLT | New Living Translation |
| NRSV | New Revised Standard Version |
| RSV | Revised Standard Version |

# 1 1 Corinthians 1:10–25

# *No Divisions among You*

You could hardly blame that motley crew of farm animals, led by an articulate pair of pigs, for conspiring to expel old Jones from his farm so they could form their own, all-animal utopian community. As George Orwell tells his classic tale, the early days of *Animal Farm* were pure bliss, with everyone working together to support the chief pigs—Snowball and Napoleon—and to resist their common (human) enemy. Before long, however, cooperation gave way to conflict. When Snowball proposed constructing a labor-saving windmill, Napoleon countered that every priority should be given to food production. While Snowball was impressing the barnyard with brilliant oratory, Napoleon was discreetly recruiting supporters one-on-one. What began as a harmonious, egalitarian community gradually split into two factions, each chanting its own slogan:

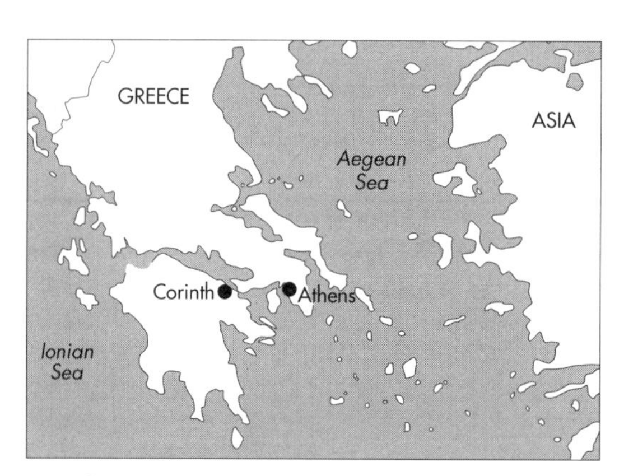

**Corinth was a coastal city in Greece.**

> "Vote for Snowball and the three-day week!"
> "Vote for Napoleon and the full manger!"

And slogans turned to battle cries, when nine canine pups, fiercely loyal to Napoleon, chased Snowball off the property and established their champion as sole director of the farm and as watch-pig of the truth. As it turned out, the real threat to the community at *Animal*

*Farm* was not 'out there' but 'in here,' in the petty disputes and divisions within the ranks of the community itself.

A similar threat hung over the Christian community in Corinth, in the early fifties of the first century. Paul describes these believers as enriched in Christ (1 Cor. 1:5) and generously gifted by the Spirit (1:7), but he also had it on good authority—from "Chloe's people" (probably a handful of slaves or employees, traveling on her behalf)—that the church in Corinth was a church divided, riven by quarrels and dissension (1:10–11). Nor was disunity simply one of many embarrassing problems Paul had to address. As we will see, it was at the root of many of their problems, and posed the single greatest threat to their very survival as the church of Jesus Christ.

So our study of First Corinthians begins with an urgent appeal for unity. No sooner has Paul delivered his opening greeting (1:1–3) and offered a prayer of thanksgiving (1:4–9) than he gets down to business. He announces the problem (1:10–12), adds an intriguing personal note (1:13–17), and then drives to the heart of the matter—the Corinthian confusion about the nature of the gospel itself (1:18–25). Each of these three sections deserves a closer look.

This was not Paul's first correspondence with Corinth (1 Cor. 5:9 may refer to a previous letter). "Some scholars believe that letter is lost without a trace. Others think it is contained in 2 Corinthians 6:14–7:1."—Barclay, *The Letters to the Corinthians,* 6.

## Tearing the Fabric (1:10–12)

The Corinthian problem was partisan politics. Christians are supposed to be cohorts, allies, teammates—"of the same mind," as Paul would say (1:10). Instead, the Corinthians were polarized and divided. Paul speaks of "schisms" in verse 10 (as well as in 11:18 and 12:25) and of public "quarrels" in verse 11. He complains again of their "quarreling," as well as "jealousy," in 3:3. If there is any good news in all of this, it is that the ecclesial fabric was still whole; rivalries *within* the church had not yet become separations *from* it. But Paul's urgings are urgent; they must stop pulling apart, start mending the tears, and find again their lost zeal for authentic community.

What would it look like, we might ask, for the Corinthians (or for us) to "be in agreement" and to "be united in the same mind" (NRSV)? Similar appeals for like-mindedness are sounded in Romans 12:16 and Philippians 2:2. Is Paul calling for lockstep uniformity? Is his goal for the church a blind, unthinking compliance to some code of beliefs and conduct? More than a few Christian groups have sought to exact this sort of absolute conformity from their members, almost always with tragic results. "Real community," as Richard John Neuhaus reminds us, "is not homogeneity. It is the discipline and devotion of disparate people bearing with one another in the hard tasks of love" (Neuhaus, 127). It would be exaggerating, but only slightly, to say that the rest of Paul's letter is a vision of Christian concord—a portrait of authentic, vibrant Christian (comm)unity in the midst of the diversity, complexity, and messiness of life.

Paul's elaborations in verse 12 add some details to our rather fuzzy picture of the church at Corinth. "Each of you says, 'I belong to Paul,' or 'I belong to Apollos,' or 'I belong to Cephas,' or 'I belong to Christ'" (1:12; cf. 3:3–6, 21). What exactly did these slogans mean? Were some Corinthians proclaiming their fierce loyalty to *Paul's* teachings, in the face of growing hostility? Did others particularly enjoy the polished style and eloquence of *Apollos* (Acts 18:24, 28)? Had some tried to pit Paul's authority against the lofty reputation of *Cephas* (a.k.a. Peter)? Did a handful of spiritual elitists in the church claim, condescendingly, to follow only *Christ?* Regrettably, our best attempts to sort out these "parties" and identify their platforms must face one simple fact: Paul is far more concerned to challenge the very idea of factions within the church than to spell out, in television talk-show detail, who thought what and why.

"Cephas is the Jewish form of Peter's name. [The followers of Cephas] were most likely Jews; and they sought to teach that a man must still observe the Jewish law."—Barclay, *The Letters to the Corinthians,* 15.

In any case, of the four names mentioned, perhaps only Paul and Apollos were rallying points for actual factions in the church, and even their supporters were probably not clearly defined and organized as parties. Paul certainly has no beef with Apollos himself; when Apollos is singled out later in the letter (3:6; 16:12), there isn't even a hint of animosity or competition. It looks as if the congregation at large, without the blessing of these high-profile leaders, had become home to cliques and splinter groups, some aligning with a big name, others perhaps dividing along house-church lines or according to race or social class.

Paul would have been deeply saddened, though perhaps not surprised, to learn that Corinth's reputation for disunity was long lived. Forty years later when Clement, Bishop of Rome, wrote to the same church, precious little seems to have changed:

> Why are there strife and passion and divisions and schisms and war among you? Or have we not one God, and one Christ, and one Spirit

> of grace poured out upon us? And is there not one calling in Christ? Why do we divide and tear asunder the members of Christ, and raise up strife against our own body, and reach such a pitch of madness as to forget that we are members one of another? . . . Your schism has turned aside many, has cast many into discouragement, many to doubt, all of us to grief; and your sedition continues. (*1 Clement* 46:5–7, 9)

How, we might ask, would Paul address the church of our day, defined as it is by denominations, politics, and personality wars? What would he say to those local congregations known more for their nasty church wars (over preaching styles, musical tastes, and building programs) than for their message of reconciliation? As Garrison Keillor puts it, the church is "cursed with a surplus of scholars and a deficit of peacemakers" (Keillor, *Leaving Home,* 155).

## Not My Department (1:13–17)

These next few verses reveal a side of Paul normally hidden from view. With eyes flashing and voice cracking, a deeply troubled apostle unleashes three rhetorically loaded questions: "Has Christ been divided? Was Paul crucified for you? Or were you baptized in the name of Paul?" (1:13). The absurdity of the questions and the structure of Paul's Greek demand strongly negative answers. Does anyone seriously imagine that Christ could be divided up and parceled out? Do some believers somehow get more of Jesus than others? Would any dare to claim that the community's life and identity derived from someone other than Christ?

> "'I belong to Christ.' Is that not what every Christian should say?"—Hays, *First Corinthians,* Interpretation, 23.

Leaving these barbs dangling in the air, Paul shifts abruptly to reminisce about the early days he spent among them (vv. 14–16). "I thank God," he declares, "that I baptized none of you except Crispus and Gaius." It was hardly a case of strategic planning on Paul's part. He had no official baptism policy at all. Only now, as he looked back, did it seem providential that he had personally baptized so few of his converts.

With verse 16 we catch Paul in the very act of writing. In the heat of the moment he has completely forgotten his baptizing "the household of Stephanas" (a group that probably included family and slaves). Perhaps we should imagine Stephanas himself, who had only recently made the journey from Corinth to Ephesus (16:17), gently jogging Paul's memory. So much had happened since the excitement of those "first converts in Achaia" (16:15)! Almost sheepishly, Paul confesses that if there *were* others, he simply can't recall.

And no wonder. As verse 17 declares, it was not Paul's mission to baptize, still less to establish his own fan club, complete with chapters in each Mediterranean seaport. Rather, Paul was "enlisted" (the verb is *apostello,* a close cousin to the noun "apostle") by Christ to "proclaim the gospel" (*euangelizo*). He was an itinerant preacher. He was a missionary. He was a point man who parachuted into enemy territory, did his job, and moved out, leaving the pastoral chores for someone else. That's why Paul normally avoided performing the initiatory rite of baptism, a rite so important to the early church (Matt. 28:19; Acts 2:41; 8:36; Rom. 6:3–7), if perhaps too important in Corinth (10:1–5; 15:29). Paul's reference to his own sense of calling, as agent of the gospel, snaps Paul out of the past and back to the present, to address their confusion over the very nature of the gospel.

"The division of the Christian communions is a scandal, and we should hear in Paul's letter to Corinth a reproach to ourselves for perpetuating this tragic state of affairs."—Hays, *First Corinthians,* Interpretation, 25.

Over the years, there has been no shortage of Christians prepared to divide over baptism, or communion, or to pledge their exclusive loyalties to some free-wheeling Christian personality, all at the expense of Christian unity. In *The Screwtape Letters,* the most popular and most haunting of C. S. Lewis's writings, we encounter a shrewd but patronizing senior devil advising his young nephew, Wormwood, on how to confound his "patient":

> I think I warned you before that if your patient can't be kept out of the Church, he ought at least to be violently attached to some party within it. I don't mean on really doctrinal issues; about those, the more lukewarm he is, the better. . . . The real fun is working up hatred between those who *say* "mass" and those who *say* "holy communion" when neither party could possibly state the difference . . . in any form which would hold water for five minutes. And all the purely indifferent things—candles and clothes and what not—are admirable ground for our activities. (Lewis, *Screwtape,* Letter XVI, page 75)

Screwtape's strategy has proven effective; "purely indifferent things" have been tearing apart Christian communities ever since—well, ever since Corinth. Incredibly, the survival of many churches today is threatened more by nasty, in-house disputes and personality wars than by external hostilities. Like Orwell's pigs, many of us prefer to drive away any members of the community whose ideas clash with our own.

## The Foolish Wisdom of God (1:18–25)

The end of verse 17, like the tail of a scorpion, hides a pointed barb. Paul contends that his preaching was not supposed to be "with eloquent wisdom" (NRSV). He was not called by Jesus Christ to hone his rhetorical skills or to transform the gospel into a clever philosophical system. He was called, on the contrary, to preach a simple, unpolished "message of the cross" (see also 2:1–5). The earliest readers of this letter would sense immediately that Paul is poised to sting those in Corinth who were inclined to put style over substance and to value human wisdom over gospel truth. By *filling* their sermons with impressive oratory and sophisticated ideas, these folks only succeed in "*emptying* the cross."

Verses 18–25 expose this Corinthian love affair with human cleverness for what it is—a stark rejection of God's way of working in the world. Those "on their way to ruin" quite naturally declare Paul's gospel to be foolishness, but we should expect those "on the way to salvation" to recognize its wisdom (1:18, NEB). Some in the Corinthian church, however, were so enamored of learning, wisdom, and philosophy that they were in danger of distorting the gospel beyond recognition.

As the quotation from Isaiah 29:14 in verse 19 reminds us, God has a long history of defying common sense (see also 1 Cor. 3:18–20). Paul's scriptures (our Old Testament) are packed with stories about God's doing something foolish or weak or backward or scandalous. Barren women deliver children (Genesis 21). Forgotten prisoners become international statesmen (Genesis 41). Reticent nomads become God's prophets (Exodus 3–4). Young shepherds found eternal dynasties (1 Samuel 16). The Bible is a book of surprise endings and dramatic reversals.

Nowhere is this more true, Paul would say, than in the events of recent history, and in the story he calls his "gospel." How can the same announcement be "sheer folly" for some and "God's power" for others (1:18, 24)? How can the way of salvation be both "wisdom" (1:24) and "foolishness" (1:21, 23, 25)? How can God's "weakness" be "stronger than human strength" (1:25)?

Paul's answer to all these questions is the same: the cross (vv. 18, 23; 2:2). On the cross we see God dramatically breaking into history. To proclaim "the message of the cross" (v. 20) is to insist, in defiance of human logic, that God has used the grisly death of Jesus to inaugurate a new age of salvation. To proclaim "Christ crucified"

(v. 23; cf. 2:2) is to declare not only that God has allowed Israel's Messiah to suffer a shameful execution, but also that Christ's humiliating defeat was (incredibly) God's glorious triumph. And so we sing with Bernard of Clairvaux:

> O sacred head, now wounded, with grief and shame weighed down;
> Now scornfully surrounded with thorns, thine only crown;
> O sacred head, what glory, what bliss till now was Thine!
> Yet, though despised and gory, I joy to call Thee mine.

> "In Jesus they saw one who was meek and lowly, one who deliberately avoided the spectacular, one who served and who ended on a Cross—and it seemed to them an impossible picture of the Chosen One of God."
> —Barclay, *The Letters to the Corinthians,* 18.

Of course, the cross was not the end of the story. Anyone who heard Paul preach would know that his gospel did not leave Jesus hanging on a cross or lying in a tomb. Certainly, Christ died for our sins and was buried, but he also rose again on the third day (1 Cor. 15:4; cf. 15:20; 6:14; 9:1) and appeared to a host of witnesses (1 Cor. 15:5-8). In fact, Paul would insist (perhaps at the top of his voice) that the story of Jesus was not even worth telling unless he really did rise from the dead: "if Christ has not been raised, your faith is futile and you are still in your sins" (1 Cor. 15:17, NRSV; cf. 15:14-19, 32; Rom. 6:4; 10:9; Phil. 2:6-11; Col. 2:12-15; 1 Thess. 1:10; 4:14). If, in the end, death conquered Jesus, there can be no hope for his followers.

But all of this makes the argument of chapter one even more intriguing. How can Paul proclaim the surpassing wisdom and power of God's salvation (1:18, 24-25) without so much as mentioning the resurrection? Why would Paul claim to preach "nothing . . . except Jesus Christ, and him crucified" (2:2)? In one sense, of course, Christ's death can never be separated from his resurrection. Those who watched Jesus die (Matt. 27:27-31; Luke 23:35-37; 24:20-21) did not find hope until they encountered him alive a few days later (Acts 2:24; 3:15; 4:10; 5:30-32; 9:40-41). Likewise Paul did not reverse his negative assessment of Jesus until he encountered him alive on the road to Damascus (1 Cor. 15:8-9; Gal. 1:11-17; cf. Acts 9:1-22).

In another sense, however, followers of Jesus can never move beyond the cross. Unlike some children's story that holds our affections for a brief time, the cross is neither preliminary nor elementary. On the contrary, the startling claim of the gospel is that the death of Jesus stands at the center of human history. Perhaps this is why the cross proved to be such an obstacle for both the Corinthian elite and for Paul's Jewish kin as well. The Greeks wanted to put something wise, something intellectually respectable at the center, but all they got was the cross, in all its foolishness and humiliation (1 Cor. 1:22-23). Meanwhile, the Jews wanted a clearer sign that God's power was at work (1:22-23), but all they could see was weakness and defeat. Stubbornly Paul insists on summing up his message with two simple words: Christ crucified (1:23; 2:2).

So even though the letter will culminate in chapter 15 with an impassioned and compelling defense of the resurrection, the focus here in chapter one is on Christ's death. This is hardly coincidental, as Hays explains: "It is no accident that his teachings on the cross (1:18-2:16) and resurrection (15:1-58) stand like bookends-or sentinels-at beginning and end of the body of his letter to the Corinthians. These are the fundamental themes of the gospel story. All our theology and practice must find its place within the world framed by these truths. (Hays, 278)

## Want to Know More?

**About the city of Corinth?** See Gerald F. Hawthorne, Ralph P. Martin, and Daniel G. Reid, *Dictionary of Paul and His Letters* (Downers Grove, Ill.: InterVarsity Press, 1993), 172–75.

**About house churches?** See William H. Willimon, *Acts,* Interpretation (Atlanta: John Knox Press, 1988), 39–42; Carolyn Osiek and David L. Balch, *Families in the New Testament World: Households and House Churches* (Louisville, Ky.: Westminster John Knox Press, 1997). For the more contemporary movement of house churches, see J. G. Davies, ed., *The New Westminster Dictionary of Liturgy and Worship* (Philadelphia: Westminster Press, 1986), 260–62.

**About Apollos?** See Hawthorne, Martin, and Reid, *Dictionary of Paul and His Letters,* 37–39.

In Tolkien's mystical tale *The Lord of the Rings,* duty compels Frodo the Hobbit and his companions to leave the sleepy Shire and set out on a dangerous quest to keep a powerful Ring from falling into the evil hands of Sauron, Lord of Mordor. As darkness falls over the land, Frodo meets with an assembly of wizards, dwarves, and elves—the Council of Elrond—to determine how, against all odds, they might elude the enemy. Two things become clear to all at that Council: that the weak and unlikely Frodo was the one to carry the Ring; and that he must carry it directly into, not away from, Mordor. As Gandalf the wizard exclaims: "It is wisdom to recognize necessity, when all other courses have been weighed, though as folly it may appear to those who cling to false

"Those who are being saved . . . recognize the cross for what it is, the power of God, and this changes the way they understand everything else."—Hays, *First Corinthians,* Interpretation, 28.

hope. Well, let folly be our cloak, a veil before the eyes of the Enemy!" With this foolish wisdom Master Elrond agreed:

> "The road must be trod, but it will be very hard. And neither strength nor wisdom will carry us far upon it. This quest may be attempted by the weak with as much hope as the strong. Yet such is oft the course of deeds that move the wheels of the world: small hands do them because they must, while the eyes of the great are elsewhere." (Tolkien 1.352–53)

Like Elrond and Gandalf, Paul knew a wisdom higher than the wisdom of the world—a wisdom that appeared pitifully weak and impossibly foolish to almost everyone else. In God's plan, of course, it was not a hobbit but a Messiah who would lay down his life, and the journey was not to Mount Doom, but to the cross.

For some of us, all this talk about God's "foolish wisdom" and "weak strength" sounds melodramatic, even unintelligible. Against the backdrop of contemporary nominal Christianity, the cross has all but lost its power to scandalize. A cross may dangle around my neck or swing from my rearview mirror, but when does it confront my intellectual conceit? or silence my incessant verbosity? If the ancients felt obliged to apologize for the cross as an embarrassment or to condemn the cross as a symbol of weakness, many today have managed to domesticate the cross as a convenient token of religiosity. Either way, it is striking how difficult it has been, through the years, for humanity to embrace the cross, humbly and quietly, as God's wise and powerful offer of salvation.

## ? Questions for Reflection

1. Paul speaks of divisions in the church at Corinth. What is his concern about these divisions? What divisions do you see in the church today? From his words to the church at Corinth, what is Paul's admonishment to us? What might we do to foster the unity in Christ that Paul speaks of?
2. Name three examples in this passage (1 Cor. 1:10–25) of foolishness? When have there been times in your life when following the will of God seemed foolish?
3. What does the phrase "the cross of Christ" mean to you? How might you explain "the cross of Christ" to a child?
4. Paul seems to be writing to a congregation that is waiting for some of its expectations of Christ to be fulfilled. What are some of your expectations of Christ?

# 2

## 1 Corinthians 3:5–17

# *God's Field and God's Temple*

This particular ghost was rather large. You might even say fat, except that he was so wispy you could see right through him. And he was clearly not impressed. His conversation partner, a dazzlingly white spirit, was urging him to journey up into the mountains, toward heaven, toward God; but the fat, thin ghost had far more interest in returning to hell, where he was scheduled (on the following Friday) to read a scholarly paper to a theological society. If he were to agree to make the journey, it could be only under certain conditions:

> "I should want a guarantee that you are taking me to a place where I shall find a wider sphere of usefulness—and scope for the talents that God has given me—and an atmosphere of free inquiry—in short, all that one means by civilization and—er—the spiritual life."
>
> "No," said the other. "I can promise you none of these things. No sphere of usefulness: you are not needed there at all. No scope for your talents: only forgiveness for having perverted them. No atmosphere of inquiry, for I will bring you to the land not of questions but of answers, and you shall see the face of God." (Lewis, *Great Divorce,* 42–43)

Although this dialogue took place only in the fertile mind of C. S. Lewis, it is all too real an indictment of many religious figures in our day. How many pastors, scholars, and Christian leaders have become drunk on the wine of their own talents and spiritual gifts? How many are addicted to the spotlight, to public recognition and applause, to the adrenaline rush that comes when others look at us and think they see greatness? And how many rank-and-file church members serving behind the scenes dream of public recognition, of "a wider sphere of usefulness"? How many of us, like the ghost, might feel somewhat ambivalent about a heaven in which we don't figure prominently as key players, or at least as honored guests?

As Paul sees it, the church at Corinth had a few too many self-appointed key players and honored guests. We saw in chapter 1 that too many of their number elevated their own wisdom over the word of the cross. Paul begins chapter 3 by taking another swipe at their partisan loyalties (3:3–4; cf. 1:11–12), but then gradually shifts to focus on the leaders themselves, on the role they play, and on the risks and rewards that go with the job. For a society like ours, led by personalities and obsessed with success, these words offer a timely and sobering reality-check.

## Team Work or Turf Wars (3:5–9a)

"What then is Apollos? What is Paul?" (v. 5). If the Corinthians are so worked up about individual leaders, they should be able to say why. Of course, Paul is not really asking them; he is ready with the answer—four answers, actually, coming in rapid fire in the space of five verses. First we're told to think of Paul and Apollos simply as "servants through whom you came to believe" (vv. 5–6, NRSV). Not *masters* but *servants.* Before long Christians would attach this term *servant* (Greek: *diakonos*) to a church office (see Phil.1:1; 1 Tim. 3:8, 12), but it began as a stock term for common laborers, like table waiters (John 2:5) and palace attendants (Matt. 22:13). Paul is not claiming elevated status but embracing lowly servility. Think of him and his colleagues in mission not as luminaries but as farmhands; not as celebrities but as chore boys going about their daily duties. Paul "planted" (for he got things started; 4:15; Acts 18:1) and Apollos "watered" (for he came along after Paul; Acts 19:1) in God's garden (v. 6).

According to verse 7, even calling them chore boys or farmhands may be assigning too much credit. Seasoned farmers know only too well that a good harvest requires what no human can provide: sun, rain, and warmth, and each at the right time. In the same way, Paul recognizes that whenever spiritual life sprouts up and flourishes, we must credit God's grace rather than human talent or coercion. Contrary to popular sentiment (and not just in Corinth), church growth is not an achievement award presented to scholars, celebrities, and pulpit heavyweights. So Paul reminds us: the church is God's work; human players are virtual nobodies. As the psalmist reminds us: "Unless the LORD builds the house, those who build it labor in vain" (Ps. 127:1, NRSV).

Verse 8 changes our angle of vision on this pair of hired hands. They are not two, Paul says, but "one." That is, their labors are interdependent and complementary, not disconnected and antagonistic. They are not adversaries in a kingdom-building contest, but teammates in a common cause. But team unity does not necessarily mean group compensation: "each one will receive personal payment for individual labor."

Finally, in verse 9, Paul and Apollos are said to be "God's fellow workers." Not coworkers with God, as the English (especially the KJV) might suggest. God doesn't need partners. These leaders are, rather, coworkers with each other under God (cf. NLT). Paul pins this term *coworker* (Greek: *synergos*) on more than a few of those who labored alongside him in the cause of Christ (e.g., 2 Cor. 8:23; Phil. 2:25; 4:3). The image is not of free-wheeling, self-employed entrepreneurs who have decided, for strategic reasons, to cooperate. Paul's vision of ministry is much more mundane, closer perhaps to our idea of employment. Imagine us, he says, as work mates losing ourselves in our jobs, looking forward to receiving our pay at the end of the day. And if we are co-laborers for God, Paul continues, then "you are God's field" where the work of the harvest takes place.

> "We are not workers with God. That is not the idea the apostle is here setting forth. We are fellow workers who belong to God, and who are working with one another."—Charles R. Erdman, *The First Epistle of Paul to the Corinthians* (Philadelphia: Westminster Press, 1966), 47.

Our greatest challenge, when faced with this passage, is not intellectual but moral. As Richard Hays acknowledges:

> It is easy to give lip service to this principle, but hard to live out its practical implications in the church. Too often clergy, rather than working cooperatively to cultivate God's field, become embroiled in turf battles. The same thing is true of other workers in the church. We all want to be sure that no one else interferes with our little patch of the field, that things are done just precisely our way. And so the field becomes endlessly subdivided into unproductive subsistence plots. (Hays, 53)

## Solid Footings or None at All (3:9b–11)

"You are God's building project." Abruptly and without warning, we leave the plantation and arrive on the construction site, where we remain throughout verses 10–15. But whether down on the farm or out on the job, the church Paul portrays belongs to God, and only to God. It does not, therefore, fall under the jurisdiction of any earthly baron or wealthy financier. This idea of divine ownership reappears with intensity later on (3:16, 23); for now Paul's thoughts take a different direction.

Far more than just the setting has changed in this section. In verses 5–9, God was the sovereign giver of life; in verses 10–15, God is the inspector and judge, dispensing fines and payments. Verses 5–9 contrast God's work with every human labor; verses 10–15 contrast wise human efforts with foolish ones. Even Paul's tone of voice has become more charged, even ominous. Readers proceed beyond this point at their own risk.

The man who comes to meet us in verse 10 is no longer Paul-the-diligent-farmhand but now Paul-the-head-contractor or chief-architect on the job. Paul's "contract" (that is, his apostolic commission) derives from "God's grace" (cf. 1 Cor.15:10; Rom.1:5; 1 Tim.1:14), and his labors are the work of a "skilled (Greek: *sophos;* wise, learned) master builder." Continuing the metaphor, Paul claims to have "laid down the foundation" of the church at Corinth. In other words, when Paul began the church, he set it down firmly on the solid footings of his apostolic gospel.

Readers of the Corinthian epistles may notice how regularly Paul reminds his readers of his apostolic status and authority (1:1; 4:9–13; 9:1–6; 14:37; 2 Cor. 3:1–3; 10:8; 11:5; 12:11–12; 13:10). He even calls himself their spiritual "father" (4:15; 2 Cor. 12:14), a claim having as much to do with authority as paternal affection. Why make such grandiose claims? Is Paul indignant because he gets no respect? Is he subtly recruiting for the "I-am-of-Paul" campaign after all (see 1:12; 3:4)? Perhaps the real reason Paul lauds himself as the "skilled master builder" comes out at the end of the verse: "each one must take care how he builds." If the church's ground floor was the careful work of a divinely commissioned apostle, it matters very much how others continue what he began. "Shoddy workmanship on top of the sound apostolic foundation is not to be tolerated" (Hays, 54).

With verse 11, Paul identifies the foundation of this building as "Jesus Christ." This can only mean the message of "Jesus Christ, and him crucified" (2:2; cf. 1:23; Eph. 2:20). Any structure not resting squarely upon, and anchored firmly to, the "word of the cross" will never pass inspection. Richard Hays paraphrases the point:

> No one can expand this foundation by saying, "Let's add on a new wing founded on wisdom," or "Let's build a new building on the foundation of scientific knowledge," or "Our contemporary religious experience requires us to dismantle the foundation and reconstruct it in a different way." (Hays, 54)

Missionaries are tempted to found churches on material handouts and relief programs. Ministers establish precarious congregations far too close to the fault lines of strategic planning, entertaining services, and winsome personalities. Churches may rest all their hopes on finding a pastor with just enough oratorical wizardry and diplomacy to distract members from each other. Sadly, in some circles, the church appears to be resting entirely on tired habits, rote formulas, and weekly routines. Thoughtful commitment to the gospel truth has slowly vanished, like the Cheshire Cat, leaving only the grin (or the grimace) of empty religion. Such churches scarcely need a future day of testing; they will crumble and collapse quite nicely on their own. Over the din of so much substandard construction we need to hear (better: sing) the timeless words of Samuel John Stone:

> "If there is and can be but one Foundation, then all persons who are united with Christ belong to the one building. There can be but one Christian church. Parties and sects are unnatural and inconsistent with a true dependence upon Christ."—Erdman, *1 Corinthians*, 50.

> The Church's one foundation is Jesus Christ, her Lord;
> She is his new creation by water and the Word:
> From heav'n he came and sought her to be his holy bride;
> With his own blood he bought her, and for her life he died.
>
> Though with a scornful wonder men see her sore oppressed,
> By schisms rent asunder, by heresies distressed,
> Yet saints their watch are keeping; their cry goes up, "How long?"
> And soon the night of weeping shall be the morn of song.

## Up in Smoke (3:12–15)

If Paul is crystal clear about the church's one foundation, he offers little help to those wanting to decipher the various building materials of verse 12: "gold, silver, precious stones, wood, hay, straw." Two points may help out. First, verse 13 suggests that we really have only two distinct categories: completely nonflammable and highly flammable. The point, surely, is that wise contractors will strictly follow the building code and use only noncombustible materials. Second, few of us can imagine building our homes out of "gold, silver, and precious stones." (Plywood, sheet rock, and concrete more readily come to mind.) Perhaps, in light of verses 16–17, Paul has in mind one particularly luxurious building project—the ongoing restoration of Herod's Temple.

It is hard to resist thinking of the proverbial Three Little Pigs at this point. As a typical folk tale, the first two episodes of that story build suspense and set the stage for the third. Thus, the first two pigs build homes of straw and of sticks (compare Paul's straw and wood), neither of which withstands the huffing and puffing of the wolf. We might say that neither pig survives the day of judgment. The third pig, of course, builds with bricks (not quite Paul's precious stones, but close); when the wolf puts the work to the test, the house survives and the pig receives her "reward." But quaint parallels sometimes conceal more fundamental contrasts. Each pig, we recall, had to build her own personal domicile, drawing upon her own personal survival skills. Each house had to endure its own day of testing. By contrast, there is only *one* church, and it rests upon only *one* foundation. As much as many of us might prefer a privatized, Three-Little-Pigs kind of religion, the church of God is profoundly communal; what we build we build together.

**The Western (or Wailing) Wall. The lower section was part of Herod's Temple.**

Hanging over all of this construction imagery is Paul's ominous warning (stated or implied six times) that the work of each builder is subject to rigorous inspection.

| | |
|---|---|
| 3:10 | "each one must take care how he builds on it" |
| 3:13 | "the work of each one will become known" |
| 3:13 | "by fire it will be revealed" |
| 3:13 | "the fire will determine the kind of work each has done" |
| 3:14 | "if the work someone has built survives, the builder will receive reward" |
| 3:15 | "if someone's work is consumed, the builder will sustain a loss" |

The building metaphor is evidently wearing rather thin; no earthly site inspector would intentionally light a fire to test for flammability! But this is because Paul's gaze is set on a future inspection day—described elsewhere as *The Day* (of Christ, of the Lord)—when God will examine all humanity, dispensing rewards and rendering judgments (Rom. 2:5, 16; 1 Cor. 1:8; 2 Cor. 1:14; Phil. 1:6, 10; 1 Thess. 5:2; 2 Thess. 1:6–10, 2 Tim. 4:8). Paul was not alone in his belief in an apocalyptic tribunal; the idea that God will one day settle the score finds support elsewhere in the New Testament (Matt. 25:31–46; John 5:25–29; 2 Pet. 3:7) and in the Hebrew prophets as well (Joel 2:30–32; Amos 5:18–20; Obad. 15–18; Mal. 4:1–3).

## Want to Know More?

**About the "Day of the Lord"?** See Shirley C. Guthrie, *Christian Doctrine,* rev. ed. (Louisville, Ky.: Westminster John Knox Press, 1994), 387–89; and William Barclay, *At the Last Trumpet: Jesus Christ and the End of Time* (Louisville, Ky.: Westminster John Knox Press, 1998), 4–17.

**About gems and precious stones in the Bible?** See Leland Ryken, James C. Wilhoit, and Tremper Longman III, *Dictionary of Biblical Imagery* (Downers Grove, Ill.: InterVarsity Press, 1998), 451–52.

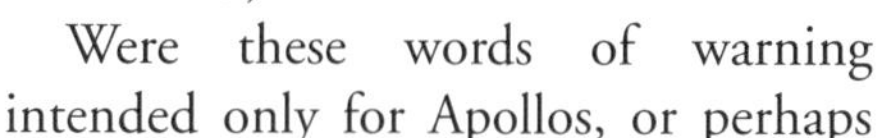

Were these words of warning intended only for Apollos, or perhaps for a handful of unnamed but prominent figures in the early church? Not if we give full weight to words like "anyone," "each one" and "no one" (used six times in verses 10–15). At the very least, the warning goes out to any and all who take part in teaching, leading, and otherwise building up the church. Today we might think of Bible study leaders and Sunday school teachers, worship planners and musicians, discipleship coordinators and lay evangelists. Anyone, in fact, who shares in the building up of the saints should take heed.

"The point is that a Christian's moral behavior affects not only the individual in question but also the Christian community of which she or he is a part. To borrow a phrase from John Donne, Paul believes that no one is an island entire in oneself. Rather, all are part of *ekklesia,* and thus what they do affects the body."—Ben Witherington, III, *Paul's Narrative Thought World: The Tapestry of Tragedy and Triumph* (Louisville, Ky.: Westminster John Knox Press, 1994), 282.

But what should these builders expect? What can it mean that certain clergy and parishioners will "receive a reward" (Greek: *misthos;* payment) on Judgment Day, whereas others "suffer loss" (Greek: *zemioo;* cf. 2 Cor. 7:9; Phil. 3:8)? As tempting as it is to read these verses individualistically, as an early version of the Three Little Pigs, we must resist. Paul is not promising eternal salvation or heavenly reward for each one who constructs his or her own personal life with the gold, silver, and precious stones of Christian virtue. As we have seen, the spotlight is less on *private* morality than on *public,* communal behavior. Divine approval awaits those who, like Paul, have labored diligently to fortify the church through sound teaching and humble acts of service. On that day, "praise will come to each one from God" (4:5; cf. 3:8). We hear a similar refrain in Jesus' parable of the talents. Those slaves who faithfully built up the king's estate during his absence hear him say: "Well done, good and faithful slave. You were faithful with a few things, I will put you in charge of many. Enter into the joy of your Lord" (Matt. 25:21, 23).

By the same token, this is not a passage promising eternal damnation for those whose personal lives are shaped by the wood, hay, and straw of private sin (but see 6:9–10). Still less is it about the purifying effects of purgatory. The warning is, rather, for those who would exchange the word of the cross for their own brilliance, or people skills, or marketplace savvy, or fund-raising expertise, or pressure tactics, or ten-year plans, or whatever. Some three hundred years ago, Philip Jacob Spener chided the "Corinthians" of his day: "Men's taste becomes accustomed to the more charming things of reason, and after a while the simplicity of Christ and his teaching appears to be tasteless" (Spener, 56).

Woe to those who serve up tasty sermonettes, who vaunt their intellectual accomplishments, who seek to improve the gospel; for they shall be sternly rebuked! It would be hard to find more apt commentary on Paul's thought than the blunt warning of James 3:1: "Not many of you should become teachers, my brothers and sisters, for you know that we who teach will be judged with greater strictness" (NRSV).

Almost reluctantly, Paul adds an important footnote at the end of verse 15: the final destiny of such shoddy builders is not on the line. By the grace of God, these characters "will be saved, but as if escaping through the fire." But the grim prospect of watching a lifetime of labor go up in flames and of entering into salvation smelling of smoke (so to speak) should sober even the most self-assured and empire-minded of Christian leaders.

"Paul uses the image of fire, a traditional Old Testament image for God's judgment."—Hays, *First Corinthians,* Interpretation, 53.

## Vandals in the Temple (3:16–17)

With verse 16 Paul adjusts, but does not entirely abandon, his building metaphor. You aren't just any old building, "you are God's temple"! It may be human leaders who build the church (3:10–15), but it is God's Spirit who indwells it (3:16–17)! In the space of two short verses, Paul advances three startling claims about the Christian community. First, Paul declares that the Corinthian church—that disheveled, diverse, and divided collection of young believers—is home to the Holy Spirit of God! The claim is not that the Spirit indwells each individual believer (though we do meet that idea later, in 1 Cor. 6:19–20; cf. Rom. 8:9–11). Rather, Paul's imagery here is corporate: the Spirit dwells among the members of the Christian community. If our modern English versions tend to obscure this point—every "you" in verses 16–17 is plural, like the old English "ye" or the southern "y'all"—the point remains too important to miss. Paul does not envision multiple private temples dotting the spiritual landscape, like the many pagan sanctuaries on display throughout Corinth or Athens, but rather a single, sacred house inhabited by a holy God. Sadly, it requires Herculean powers of imagination for many of us to envision the church in all its "sweaty, smelly concreteness" (Neuhaus, 10) as a consecrated, spiritual temple. As Charles Colson quips, onlookers are more likely to be reminded of "a gigantic flea market with the vendors competing against one another, hawking their wares in a huge, discordant din" (Colson, 72).

A second claim, tied to the first, is that the predominantly Gentile church has taken over the role filled for so many years by the Jewish Temple at Jerusalem! No longer must God's people climb the winding road to Mount Zion to offer their worship and praise. "The Spirit of God no longer can be localized in a sacred building," Hays explains. "It is to be found in the gathered community of God's elect people in Christ" (Hays, 57). If God's Spirit is indeed present in our midst, then "we are the temple of the living God" (2 Cor. 6:16; see also Eph. 2:21–22 and 1 Peter 2:5). Many of Paul's Jewish contemporaries, no doubt raised on stories about the Temple (e.g., 1 Kings 5–6; 1 Chronicles 22; 2 Chronicles 2–7; Ezra 5–6), would hotly contest his implicit rejection of Jerusalem's privileged status (see John 4:21–24; Acts 6:13; 7:48; 22:28).

"As Christians live in the Spirit and in Christ, so we can also say that Christ is in the believer (Gal. 2:20; Rom. 8:10) or the Spirit lives in the believer (Rom. 8:9, 11). As Christians are supposed to walk in love, so is God's love poured into their hearts (Rom. 5:5). Thus outside and inside, living space and inhabitant can be exchanged."—Jürgen Becker, *Paul: Apostle to the Gentiles* (Louisville, Ky.: Westminster John Knox Press, 1993), 418.

Third, Paul issues a dire warning: "If anyone destroys (Greek: *phtheiro;* ruins, corrupts) God's temple, God will destroy (*phtheiro* again) that person" (NRSV). The punishment will fit the crime. But what exactly was the crime, and who were the criminals? As part of Paul's sustained attack on divisions, parties, and strife in the church, the target of this threat must be those who work to undermine the precious (and often precarious) unity of the church. Whether or not Paul had in mind a few particularly quarrelsome members of the Corinthian church, the threat of eternal punishment is genuine. Shoddy, second-rate church-*builders* may escape through the flames (3:15), but church-*destroyers* will have no such luck. Those among us who display a casual acceptance of jealousy, gossip, petty rivalry, and one-upmanship should remember that although Christ promised to build and protect his church (Matt.16:18), he nowhere promised similar protection for those who deliver blow after blow against it.

The admonition is haunting. Shoppers for an older house long to hear the building inspector declare that "the foundations are sure," for a house resting on shifting or fractured footings cannot endure. Should not we who call the church our "home" be even more concerned about its foundations?

## Questions for Reflection

1. Paul describes himself as more of a farmhand or chore boy. Christians would later attach the term "servant" (*diakonos*) to a church office. What do you think about when you think of an officer? Compare and contrast your concepts of a servant with that of an officer.
2. According to Paul, the foundation of the church is Jesus Christ. He goes on to say that as we build God's church, we have to use the "right stuff." What might be this "right stuff"? How does one cultivate the "right stuff"?
3. Paul states that the Holy Spirit dwells in us both as believers and in Christian community. What are some of the indications of the presence of the Spirit? What other scriptures can you think of that speak of the presence of the Holy Spirit?
4. Paul has a strict warning for those he calls "temple destroyers." What do you think Paul is speaking about? Who or what are the destroyers?

# 1 Corinthians 5:1–13

# 3

## *Hand Over to Satan*

Shock waves rolled across the city of Corinth. People everywhere were asking, "Did he really marry the wife of his dead father? How could such a shameful thing happen to one of us?" The man at the center of the scandal was Oedipus. Although he had grown up in the palace of King Polybus of Corinth, his true father was King Laius of Thebes. As the story goes, King Laius abandoned Oedipus as an infant after hearing an oracle foretelling his own death at the hands of his son. But Queen Jocasta succumbed to maternal instincts and rescued Oedipus, sending him away with a shepherd who eventually brought the lad to Corinth where he was taken in by the royal family there. Years later, Oedipus himself would learn that he was fated to kill his father and marry his mother. This discovery compelled him to flee from the couple he thought were his parents, only to encounter his real father without knowing it. As fate would have it, Oedipus and Laius came to blows and only Oedipus survived. From there he advanced to Thebes, where he took the newly widowed Queen Jocasta as his bride, unaware that she was also his mother.

Years passed before the details of the scandal came together. As Sophocles tells the tale, Oedipus first heard the sordid truth from the reluctant lips of a blind seer named Teiresias. "You have been living in unguessed shame with your nearest kin," he declares, "and do not see to what woe you have come." When the truth could no longer be ignored, Oedipus' tormented mother ends her own life. As for Oedipus, he savagely puts out his eyes and then pleads that others would drive him away into exile:

> Haste, lead me from the land, friends, lead me hence, the utterly lost, the thrice accursed, yea, the mortal most abhorred of heaven! . . . Cast

me out of this land with all speed, to a place where no mortal shall be found to greet me more. (Sophocles, *Oedipus Rex*)

The tragic tale of *Oedipus Rex* would have captivated generations of Corinthian children. If they marveled at the legendary exploits of Hercules or the matchless beauty of Helen, they would also have recoiled at the dreadful crimes of a man who murdered his father and married his mother. Even in Paul's day, when moral standards in places like Corinth were notoriously lax, most people would cringe at the thought of such incestuous affairs. Most people would recoil, but apparently not everyone. At least one group within Corinth boasted a more enlightened, tolerant point of view. That group was the Christian church; we find their story in 1 Corinthians 5.

## Living in "Unguessed Shame" (5:1–5)

Word has made its way across the Aegean Sea to Ephesus (cf. 1:11) that sexual misconduct has infiltrated the Corinthian church. "It is actually reported that there is sexual immorality among you" (5:1). We must not imagine that Paul is embarrassed simply because a properly private matter has been leaked to the public (for that problem, see 6:1–8). Rather, his outrage is directed at the sin itself—sexual immorality (Greek: *porneia*). Elsewhere the phrase covers a range of misdeeds (cf. 6:13, 18; 7:2; 2 Cor. 12:21; Gal. 5:19; Eph. 5:3; Col. 3:5; 1 Thess. 4:3); here it clearly refers to a man who "has his father's wife."

> "The word *ethnē*, translated by NRSV and most English versions as "pagans," is Paul's normal word for "Gentiles" (i.e., non-Jews). His use of this term here offers a fascinating hint that he thinks of the Gentile converts at Corinth as Gentiles no longer."—Hays, *First Corinthians*, Interpretation, 81.

If most of the nasty details are lost to us, three points are not. First, this wife was not the man's birth mother, but a subsequent wife of his father (who may have been dead, divorced, or still around). Second, she was not a part of the church (for Paul has nothing to say about her). Third, the son and stepmother were involved sexually (the Greek word translated "has" or "living with" is a loaded term). Sophocles called it "unguessed shame." "An abomination!" cries Moses (Lev. 18:26). As for Paul, he caustically points out that this sort of corruption was "not found even among pagans" (NRSV; 5:1b). It is one thing to find behavior in the church that law-observant Jews wouldn't tolerate (see Deut. 27:20; Lev. 18:8; 20:11), but it is something else entirely when moral standards within the church sink lower than those in the world outside.

"The behavior of the incestuous man is a direct violation of God's covenant norms for Israel."—Hays, *First Corinthians,* Interpretation, 81.

With verse 2, Paul exposes a second reason for his outrage—the response of the community. Remarkably, Paul is even more agitated by the group's attitude than by the individual's sin. "And you are arrogant!" he cries (cf. 4:6, 18–19). Rather than mourn and expel the sinner, you've made this a reason to "boast" (v. 6)! Verse 2 presents a bit of a puzzle. Was the congregation proud because of or in spite of the offense of the individual member? Was Paul opposing their cool tolerance of the man's behavior? (Their modern counterparts chirp, "no one's perfect, just forgiven.") Or were they actually encouraging this character in his sinful ways (proudly proclaiming, "all things are lawful"; cf. 6:12)? Perhaps the sinner was a wealthy patron whom the church could ill afford to alienate (a problem entirely foreign to modern Christians, of course).

Whatever their attitude, whether nonchalance or arrogance, Paul pronounces the community no longer free to ignore the problem and commands them to remove the offender from their midst. As Hays explains: "Paul insists that the community has moral responsibility for the conduct of its members and that the conduct of the individual members (even private conduct between 'consenting adults') affects the life of the whole community" (Hays, 82). This is a tough one for a privatized, individualized, do-it-yourself, personal-pan-pizza society like ours to swallow. We identify more readily with the detachment and isolation captured by songwriter Paul Simon's sardonic claim to be "a rock" and "an island."

With verses 3–5, we arrive at the heart of Paul's word to the community. He cannot be there in person, but that does not stop him from pronouncing judgment on the perpetrator (v. 3) and doing so "in the name (= authority) of the Lord Jesus." Our English versions do not all agree on where to divide the clauses of verses 3 and 4. The New Jerusalem Bible, for example, reads: "When you have gathered *together in the name of our Lord Jesus . . .*" (cf. NEB, NIV; Matt. 18:20). But it is probably better to read these words as part of Paul's stunning claim to be acting, as an apostle, on the Lord's behalf (RSV, NRSV, NLT).

As for the Corinthian church, Paul is uncomfortably specific: "When you are assembled, and my spirit is present with the power of the Lord Jesus, you are to hand this man over to Satan for the destruction of the flesh, so that his spirit may be saved in the day of the Lord" (5:4–5 NRSV). These are hard words—rather intolerant, you might say—which is why generations of Christians have wondered whether, and how, the church might put them into practice. One thing is clear: Paul envisions a Christian community empowered by the risen Christ, experiencing the moving of the Spirit, and authorized to do major spiritual housecleaning. For those whose church operates more like a country club (or theater company, or funeral parlor, or volunteer center), little of Paul's address will make sense.

Paul calls this church to "hand this man over to Satan." Some have suggested that Paul wanted a curse pronounced over the culprit, but the apostle is more likely calling them, in graphic language, to expel and publicly exclude the man from the community, placing him "outside the sphere of God's redemptive protection" (Hays, 85; cf. 1 Tim. 1:20; Job 2:4–6). This is not the first century equivalent to having someone step down from a few church committees. Nor does this resemble a polite request for a letter of resignation. Rather, the gist of this passage is that the Corinthians were being told not to associate with him or even eat with him (5:11; 2 Thess. 3:14). Soberly and prayerfully, they were to close ranks and exclude the sinner from their common life, their corporate gatherings and shared meals. No more potlucks. No more prayer breakfasts. No more Holy Communion. The command was, in other words, to banish this man from the one community that provided his spiritual shelter and guidance, and to thrust him out into the world.

> "It was discipline, not exercised solely to punish, but rather to awaken; and was a verdict to be carried out, not with cold, sadistic cruelty, but rather in sorrow as for one who had died."—Barclay, *The Letters to the Corinthians*, 44.

It is fruitful to compare these verses with Jesus' instructions found in Matthew 18:15–20. Unlike the scene in 1 Corinthians 5, the sin of Matthew 18 starts out private and personal, and becomes public only when all else fails. But Matthew and Paul both agree that (a) the Christian community (b) possesses Jesus' authority (c) to expel the impenitent sinner, and Matthew's call to treat him "as a Gentile and a tax collector" may be quite close (from a Jewish-Christian perspective) to Paul's "hand this man over to Satan."

However harsh, radical, and intolerant Paul may appear, he was not advocating mere retribution. The call was for stern discipline, but not vindictive retaliation. Notice carefully how verse 5 unfolds: "hand this man over to Satan *for the destruction of the flesh, so that his spirit may be saved in the day of the Lord*" (NRSV). Some think that Paul expected Satan to rain down physical affliction or death upon the one being disciplined (cf. 1 Cor. 11:30; Acts 5:1–11). But there are good reasons to understand "destruction of the flesh," not as Paul's code for physical death, but as shorthand for a dramatic reversal of this man's spiritual direction. His "flesh" or "sinful nature" (NIV, NLT) will be chastened, reproved, "crucified" (Gal. 5:24; 6:14; cf. Rom. 6:12–14). There will be, Paul hopes, genuine remorse, tearful repentance, inner transformation, and joyful restoration to the community. This is precisely what we see in 2 Corinthians 2:5–11 and 7:10. Whether or not these verses provide the hopeful sequel to the story of 1 Corinthians 5, they certainly show how profoundly Paul believed that church discipline should lead to forgiveness and restoration.

## A New Exodus (5:6–8)

Imagine a batch of dough that remains unchanged by "a little leaven." We may as well envision a patient unbothered by "a little cancer" or an arctic explorer scoffing at "a little gangrene." Leaven leavens. Infections fester. Sin permeates. To tolerate even one defiantly sinful church member is to contaminate the entire assembly.

On first reading, we might take verse 6 as a merely poetic interlude, a dash of proverbial insight coming from the kitchen (cf. Gal. 5:9). But Paul could scarcely speak of unleavened bread without recalling a story—the story of Israel's miraculous liberation from Egyptian bondage (Exodus 11–12). Each year, in memory of that event, the Israelites would empty their homes of leaven at the beginning of the seven-day Feast of Unleavened Bread (Ex. 12:15, 19; Deut. 16:4). They did this to recall that final night in Egypt when their ancestors prepared a meal of lamb, bitter herbs, and bread. There was no time to watch the dough rise; they had to eat it "in haste" and be ready to move out at a moment's notice (Ex. 12:11, 33–39).

> Borrowing from the Passover imagery, the lamb (Christ) has been sacrificed, "so the time is at hand for the Corinthians to carry out the other major part of the festival, searching out and removing all 'leaven' (symbolizing the wrongdoer) from their household (Ex. 12:15)."—Hays, *First Corinthians*, Interpretation, 83.

Like Israel of old, Paul says, Christians are to "clean out the old leaven" and "celebrate the festival . . . with the unleavened bread of sincerity and truth" (5:7–8 NRSV). On one level, this is yet another call for spiritual housecleaning; the sinner in question must be swept up and put out of the church. But there's more. When the Israelites slaughtered the lamb for that last supper in Egypt, they were instructed to smear its blood on their doorposts and lintels as a sign of God's protection against "the destroyer" who was coming to strike down every firstborn (Ex. 12:7, 12–13, 22–27). All those who took shelter under the blood would be spared. So Paul's bold metaphor invites the new Israel to look back to her own Passover, her own exodus, her own liberation: "For our paschal lamb, Christ, has been sacrificed" (5:7 NRSV). At the center of the feast that Christians celebrate is Christ, whose death, like the death of the unblemished Passover lamb, brings life. As Richard Hays explains: "In the church we are protected from destruction by Christ's death, set free from the power that held us captive, and sent out on a journey toward a promise" (Hays, 91).

"For our paschal Lamb, Christ, has been sacrificed."

## A Double Standard? (5:9–13)

There has been some mistake. In an earlier letter (which has not survived), Paul spelled out his policy of separation from reckless sinners in the church. But some at Corinth misunderstood (or misrepresented) him to be calling for a general separation from all sinners everywhere. "Nonsense," says Paul, "for then you would have to leave the world!" (5:10).

> The fact that Paul regards this suggestion as self-evidently ridiculous shows that his vision for the church is not isolationist. His communities live and work in the midst of the thriving cities of the Hellenistic Mediterranean world, seeking to live as a prophetic counterculture in the midst of an unbelieving world. His concern is that the church must truly be a counterculture, rather than becoming indistinguishable from the world around it. (Hays, 87)

Paul advocates, in other words, a double standard: meaningful engagement with sinful, non-Christian neighbors, but vigilant separation from any "brother" or "sister" who persists in sinful practices that bring shame to the name of Christ. *In* the world, but not *of* the world, Jesus would say (John 17:13–18). Some of the Corinthians appear to have confused the "in" and the "of," adopting (or promoting) the ways of the world while advocating the strictest separation from it. As John Fischer laments, this in/of confusion persists to our day.

The In's and Out's of It

"In it, not of it," the statement was made as Christian One faced the world, much afraid.
"In it, not of it," the call was made clear, but Christian One got something stuck in his ear.
"Not in it, or of it" was the thing that he heard. And knowing the world was painfully absurd,
He welcomed the safety of pious retreat, and went to the potluck for something to eat.

Now Christian Two, he knew what to do, he'd show those fundies a thing or two!
How will the world ever give Christ a try if we don't get in there and identify?
So "In it, and of it," he said in his car, as he pulled in and stopped at a popular bar.
"I'll tell them the truth as soon as I'm able to get myself out from under this table."

Now along comes Christian Three jogging for Jesus, in witnessing sweats made of four matching pieces.
His earphones are playing a hot Christian tune about how the Lord is coming back soon.
"Not in it, but of it," he turns down the hill and stops in for a bite at the Agape Grill.
Like the gold on the chain of his "God Loves You" bracelet, he can have the world without having to face it.

While way up in heaven they lament these conditions that come from changing a few prepositions.
"Not in it, or of it," Christian One thought. But who in the world will know that he's not?
"In it, and of it," thought Christian Two. But who in the world will know that he knew?

"Not in it, but of it," thought Christian Three. But who in the world watches Christian TV?

And Jesus turns to Gabriel, shaking His head. " 'In it, not of it,' wasn't that what I said?"

(Fischer, 132–33)

Paul does not itemize vices in verses 10 and 11 in order to eliminate the need for careful discernment and agonizing prayer. To be sure, each misdeed on the list calls for sober reflection, especially because some, like greed, are woven so tightly into the fabric of Western society. Others, like idolatry, will return to haunt us later in the letter (10:7, 14–22). But discipline in the church can never be automatic, as if checklists and church handbooks can replace the wisdom and work of the Spirit in the community. Even Paul's swift and strict approach to the egregious case of incest should not be transformed into a new law to be mechanically applied without further ado.

Verse 12 underscores that discipline belongs in-house: "is it not those within [the church] whom you judge?" (5:12). As throughout the chapter, Paul's central concern is to purify the community rather than to punish the individual. So, when he punctuates his address in verse 13 with a forceful refrain from Deuteronomy (found in 17:7; 19:19; 22:21, 24; see also 13:5; 17:12), he is not so much interested in highlighting the wickedness of the individual sinner. He is burdened to charge the church to take whatever drastic measures are necessary to fulfill its calling as God's holy, new covenant people.

"The six items in Paul's list are closely correlated with six passages in Deuteronomy that call for the penalty of death."—Hays, *First Corinthians,* Interpretation, 87.

## Exit or Exile?

For a variety of reasons, the modern church is at least as reluctant as its Corinthian counterpart to discipline deviant members—perhaps more so. Some have redefined Christian love in terms of unqualified acceptance. As Hays observes, refusal to discipline "is often justified in the name of enlightened tolerance of differences, but in fact 'tolerance' can become a euphemism for indifference and lack of moral courage" (Hays, 89). Others are so fiercely individualistic that they wouldn't dream of rendering any kind of moral judgment upon someone else.

Even when discipline does take place (amidst tears, and fears of costly lawsuits, and unsympathetic media attention), the excluded member is often welcomed—sometimes even recruited or hired—by the church down the road. Or, perhaps worse, he simply carries on, by himself, with only the slightest twinges of regret or sense of loss. As long as our relationships are thin and superficial, our worship feeble, and our prayers and teaching trite, we should not expect banished sinners to come crawling back pleading for forgiveness and restoration. They may simply discover they have more spare time on their hands. Sunday morning is an ideal tee time.

On the other hand, for those who have come to experience the church as their true home—a haven in the storm, a sanctuary of rest, a source of life and strength—exclusion would bring terrible pain. Ask Adam and Eve how they felt to be driven away from the only home they knew (Gen. 3:24). Or ask their son Cain (Gen. 4:12–14), or Hagar, Sarah's maiden (Gen. 21:14–16). What was it like for Jacob to spend the best years of his life in self-imposed exile (Gen. 27:41–46; 32:7, 11)? How would Joseph describe being sold into slavery and carted off to a strange land (Gen. 37:18–36)? Ask David about life on the run (1 Sam. 27:1; 30:3–6; cf. Psalm 142). Ask Israel how it felt to be "handed over" to invading Babylonian hordes and cast into exile (Psalm 137; Habakkuk 1).

## Want to Know More?

**About Satan?** See Guthrie, *Christian Doctrine,* 166–91, esp. 179–82.

**About excommunication?** See Richard P. McBrien, *The HarperCollins Encyclopedia of Catholicism* (San Francisco: Harper, 1996), 500–501.

**About Passover?** See James D. Newsome, *Exodus,* Interpretation Bible Studies (Louisville, Ky.: Geneva Press, 1998), 37–48; For the history of Passover, see Werner H. Schmidt, *The Faith of the Old Testament: A History* (Philadelphia: Westminster Press, 1983), 119–23. For how Passover is observed today, see Celia Brewer Marshall, *A Guide through the Old Testament* (Louisville, Ky.: Westminster John Knox Press, 1989), 45–46.

**About the number of possible letters written to Corinth?** See Celia Brewer Marshall, *A Guide through the New Testament* (Louisville, Ky.: Westminster John Knox Press, 1994), 84–85; also Roetzel, *The Letters of Paul,* 83–96.

If anyone in our day has known the terror of being driven from safety into the sinister realm of Satan, it was Elie Wiesel. In 1944, fifteen-year-old Elie, along with his father and his entire community, was deported from his native Romania to a Nazi concentration camp in Buchenwald. Ten days and nights in an open boxcar, in the dead of winter, without food or water, feeding only on the snow that never stopped falling. In *Night,* his first book, Wiesel recalls the horrors of those first few days in exile:

> When at last a gray glimmer of light appeared on the horizon, it revealed a tangle of human shapes, heads sunk upon shoulders, crouched, piled one on top of the other, like a field of dust-covered tombstones in the first light of the dawn. I tried to distinguish those who were still alive from those who had gone. But there was no difference. (Wiesel)

Young Elie found himself inhabiting, quite literally, the realm of death. He was an exile in a world held captive to evil. Incredibly, he survived every Nazi atrocity (at Buchenwald and three other camps) and grew up to wage his own war against oppression and violence, winning a Nobel Prize in 1986 for his efforts.

What if every church truly was a haven of protection and shelter in a spiritually hostile world? What if the Christian community consistently, patiently shielded the vulnerable and nourished the weak? What if the people of God ministered healing and wholeness to one another, day after day? Might not exclusion from a community like that feel like exile? Like boarding a train to a death camp? Perhaps the prospect of separation from that kind of church—of being "handed over to Satan"—would drive sinners toward repentance, and all of us toward holiness.

## ? Questions for Reflection

1. Paul advocates church discipline in this passage. How can this be balanced with the scriptures about grace? Even today, what are ways the church has responsibility for her members?
2. The writer of this study suggests we should live *in* the world without being *of* the world. What distinction is being made in this phrase? How easy is it to live in the tensions of this distinction?
3. In 5:3 Paul mentions that though he is absent in body, he is "present in spirit." What do you think this means? Paul also uses the word "spirit" in 2:4, and again in 5:5. How is Paul changing the meaning of this word?
4. What would it take to make the church "a haven of protection and shelter in a spiritually hostile world"?

# 1 Corinthians 7:1–40 4

## *Marriage and Divorce*

"**B**y the time you receive this, we'll be gone—several dozen of us. We came from the Level Above Human in distant space and we have now exited the bodies that we were wearing for our earthly task, to return to the world from whence we came—task completed." So begins a public statement, released in late March of 1997 by thirty-nine members of a group known as Heaven's Gate. Theirs was certainly no normal exit. The plan was to rendezvous, as disembodied souls, with an alien ship trailing behind comet Hale-Bopp. But for that to happen, the faithful would need to leave behind everything from this world—absolutely everything. Members shunned outsiders (including family) and lived together in celibacy and poverty. Then, on the grounds of their posh estate in Rancho Santa Fe, California, they ingested massive doses of the sedative phenobarbital (mixed with applesauce and washed down with 100-proof vodka), secured plastic bags over their heads, and lay down to die.

What would drive this little cluster of people—roughly the size of a first-century house church—to commit mass suicide? The answer comes in an earlier statement from the group: "the earth's present 'civilization' is about to be recycled—'spaded under'—in order that the planet might be refurbished. The human 'weeds' have taken over the garden and disturbed its usefulness beyond repair." In other words, members of Heaven's Gate firmly believed in the imminent end of the present world order. To them, these are the "last days." And those convictions radically shaped and directed the way they lived—and the way they died.

Anyone who ponders the doctrines of Heaven's Gate and then turns to 1 Corinthians 7 may suddenly experience *déjà vu.* Consider the following remarks: "I mean, brothers and sisters, the appointed time has grown short; from now on, let even those who have wives be as though they had none, and those who mourn as though they were not mourning, and those who rejoice as though they were not rejoicing, and those who buy as though they had no possessions, and those who deal with the world as though they had no dealings with it. For the present form of this world is passing away" (7:29–31, NRSV).

Paul was certainly *not* waiting for an alien craft to whisk him away along with his fellow disciples (although some have read 1 Thess. 4:15–18 along those lines). Nor, of course, was he advocating suicide (not even in Phil. 1:21–23). But Paul did insist that the time was short—that the day of the Lord was drawing nearer all the time (see 1:7–8; 3:12–15; 4:5; 5:5; 10:11). As we witness the proliferation of doomsday cults at the dawn of yet another Christian millennium, it is tempting to disavow Paul's end-times urgency. But whatever our reaction to Paul's "last days" frame of mind, it is very clear from 1 Corinthians 7 that Paul's hope for the future profoundly informed and shaped his moral vision for the Christian present.

To understand fully the mass suicide of Heaven's Gate, we must try to view the world through their eyes and, if only for a moment, "believe" in their doomsday predictions and intergalactic soul travel. Likewise, to make sense of Paul's revolutionary advice on matters of sex and marriage, as outlined in 1 Corinthians 7, we must enter fully into his thought world and embrace his eager expectation of the Lord's return. Can that be done? What would it mean for us to allow that eager expectation to shape our lives and influence our choices? What would it mean if we don't?

## Marital IOU (7:1–7)

Paul's topic in this chapter is not of his own choosing. As the opening line indicates, the Corinthians had written to him on a range of topics including marriage (7:1–40) and idol meat (8:1–11:1), and perhaps also spiritual gifts (12:1–14:40), money (16:1–4), and the resurrection (15:1–58). Whether they wrote to pose urgent questions or rather to challenge Paul's authority (possibly disputing points in his earlier letter; see 5:9–11) remains obscure. Either way, we are wise to keep in mind that much of chapters 7–16 is really one half of a two-way conversation.

Nowhere is this more true than right there in 7:1, with the words "It is well for a man not to touch a woman" (NRSV). These remarks sound like a promotional slogan for sexual abstinence, especially because "touch" is almost certainly a euphemism for intercourse (rather than marriage, as in the NIV; cf. Gen. 20:6; Prov. 6:29). Small wonder philosopher Bertrand Russell complained that "the worst feature of the Christian religion . . . is its attitude toward sex" (Russell, 26)! But before we accuse Paul of excessive prudery, we should ask, "Whose slogan is it?" Was Paul repeating himself from an earlier letter? Or were these words, as Richard Hays suggests, "a direct citation from the Corinthians' letter, or at least a pithy summary of one of its main points" (Hays, 113)? (Note that the NRSV encloses these words in quotation marks; see also 6:12–13; 8:1, 4.)

> "The curious way that Paul argues in this chapter, qualifying rather than contradicting their positions, suggests that he may well have said something in Corinth in support of the celibate life."—Jouette M. Bassler, "1 Corinthians," in *Women's Bible Commentary: Expanded Edition,* ed. Carol A. Newsom and Sharon H. Ringe (Louisville, Ky.: Westminster John Knox Press, 1998), 413.

Whether or not verse 1 trumpets a Corinthian "slogan," verse 2 shows that Paul is not quite ready to embrace their campaign: "But because of cases of sexual immorality, each man should have his own wife and each woman her own husband" (7:2, NRSV). These remarks are commonly treated as practical, candid advice to singles: "Celibacy may be ideal, but it's not very practical. If you really want to avoid sexual sin, you should get married." This reading has the advantage of taking Paul's words at face value, but it has serious problems explaining why Paul advises against getting married later in the chapter (7:25–26, 32–34). It is probably better to read the word "have" in verse 2 as a delicate reference to sexual relations (much like 5:1; cf. Ex. 2:1; Deut. 28:30) and to take all of verses 1–7 as Paul's advice for those already married. Married couples, Paul declares, "must not declare a moratorium on sexual relations" (Hays, 116).

Whichever way we read verse 2, verses 3–5 repeatedly challenge each partner to fulfill the other's sexual needs. No doubt many ancient readers (and, alas, many moderns) would find Paul's emphasis on mutual obligation troubling. Feel free, Paul, to remind *her* she belongs to *him,* but don't bother to reverse the pronouns! But the apostle is adamant: the husband is likewise indebted sexually to his wife (v. 3), and the wife has authority over her husband's body (v. 4). Not that Paul is inviting partners to treat each other as objects. Au contraire. As Gordon Fee points out, the stress is not on "You owe me," but on "I owe you" (Fee, 280).

For many of us the obvious puzzler is why anyone would need such advice. Are we seriously to believe that some in Corinth were advocating marriage without sex? Apparently, yes. In their zeal to walk in the Spirit, to attain higher levels of wisdom, spirituality, and holiness (2:6, 15; 3:1; 7:34; 8:1–2), some appear to have renounced sex—even marital sex—as fleshly and unspiritual. Maybe this is what had driven some men in the church to seek release among prostitutes (6:12–20). In any case, as Hays reminds us, "this sort of asceticism was 'in the air' in ancient Mediterranean culture" (Hays, 114). Stoic and Cynic pundits could wax eloquent on the superiority of singleness; Rome's Vestal Virgins were thought to wield spiritual power on the city's behalf; and, among the Jews, at least some Essenes lived in the desert, renounced marriage, and lived a strict, monastic life. We can even point to pockets of asceticism in the early church (Col. 2:20–23; 1 Tim. 4:3).

The only exception to Paul's rule comes in verse 5: "Stop depriving one another, except perhaps by mutual agreement for a time so as to devote yourselves to prayer, and then be together again." Through the years thoughtful Christians have recognized the value of periods of abstinence within marriage. In *The Spirit of the Disciplines,* Dallas Willard observes how "absolutely vital to the health of any marriage" it is "that sexual gratification not be placed at the center. Voluntary abstention helps us appreciate and love our mates as whole persons, of which their sexuality is but one part" (Willard, 170). These are wise words, but not quite Paul's point, which really comes at the end of verse 5: "so that Satan may not tempt you because of your lack of self-control" (NRSV). Paul *permits*—he does not *command*—temporary and mutually acceptable abstinence, in conjunction with a focused time of disciplined prayer. But as verse 6 makes clear, within marriage abstinence should be the exception, not the rule. If God had "gifted" Paul to find fulfillment in a life of disciplined celibacy (v. 7), and if that life brought certain advantages (see 7:28, 32–35), Paul also recognized that only those similarly gifted should endeavor to follow his example.

## Single or Married—Everyone Stay Put (7:8–11)

After hinting at his preference for singleness (v. 7), Paul turns his attention toward "the unmarried and the widows." Because "widow" refers to a woman who has lost her husband, Paul may be using the term "unmarried" for men in a similar situation—those we call widowers. (If so, his attention doesn't turn to "virgins," the never-before-married, until verse 25.) It is best, Paul says, for those who have been bereaved to remain, like me, unattached (cf. 7:39–40). (Many think these remarks imply that Paul himself had previously been married.) Remain unattached, like me, unless you are "not practicing self-control" (v. 9). As Hays explains, "Paul is concerned that widowers or widows might find themselves lured into illicit sexual activity (perhaps with prostitutes or in extramarital affairs)" (Hays, 119). For those lacking continence, "it is better to marry than to burn" (v. 9, NASV).

The last line of verse 9 has sometimes been read as a threat: those who practice illicit sex can expect the flames of judgment (cf. NJB; 1 Cor. 3:15; 6:9–10). But Paul's flow of thought here (esp. 7:2, 5, 7) and his similar diction elsewhere (2 Cor. 11:29) suggest that we should think rather of the inner "flames" of unchecked sexual passion (see NRSV, NIV, NEB, NLT; cf. Sirach 23:16). So, Paul says, if you are able to remain pure, remain single.

This remain-as-is refrain echoes throughout the chapter (see vv. 10, 17, 20, 24, 26, 40), so it must be important. Singles should stay single; couples should stay coupled; virgins should stay virgin; everyone, it seems, should stay put—all of which raises the pressing question: Why does Paul appear so stubbornly committed to the status quo? More on that later.

With verses 10 and 11, Paul turns back to "the married," but his topic shifts from sex to divorce. When Paul says "I give this command—not I but the Lord" (NRSV), he is appealing directly to Jesus' teaching on the subject (cf. Matt. 5:31–32 and Luke 16:18; Mark 10:2–12 and Matt. 19:3–12). Whether this appeal is an afterthought ("come to think of it, Jesus said the same thing") or carefully premeditated, it shows that Paul was aware of Jesus' divorce sayings and considered them relevant and authoritative. (For other explicit appeals to sayings of Jesus, see 1 Cor. 9:14; 11:23; 1 Tim. 5:18.) It also suggests that verses 10–11 envision both partners belonging to the covenant community—what we might call a "Christian" marriage. "Mixed" marriages (with only one believing partner) do not come into view until verse 12.

> "Although the wording here is different from that found in the Gospels, Paul is certainly alluding to the tradition that Jesus had forbidden divorce . . . , an unusual stance more stringent than anything found either in Judaism or in Greco-Roman culture."—Hays, *First Corinthians,* Interpretation, 120.

The message is clear: neither husband nor wife should seek to end the marriage. Just Say No. Paul's earliest readers, like the earliest followers of Jesus, would have considered this no-divorce stance remarkably hard-line (cf. Matt. 19:10). Among Jews, men (but only men) had considerable freedom to end their marriages; in the Roman world, either spouse could and did take the initiative to divorce. And with the upper classes, divorce was almost fashionable. Among Christians, Paul says, things should be different. Once again, the guiding principle is to stay put. Remain together. Don't cut the knot.

But if Paul is a hard-liner, he is also a realist. He knows that some will inevitably opt out of marriage. Perhaps some Corinthian Christians already had. In that case, "if she does separate, let her remain unmarried or else be reconciled to her husband" (7:11a, NRSV). In other words, Paul, like Jesus before him, believed marriage was for keeps (1 Cor. 7:39; Rom. 7:1–3; Mark 10:9), but if divorce did happen, remarriage to another partner was out. As Hays observes, the underlying principle may be that "divorcing one spouse to marry another is nothing other than a legalized form of adultery" (Hays, 120; cf. Mark 10:11–12).

This is where things get sticky for many Christians in our no-fault divorce, serial-marriage society. For us, Paul's counsel is double-edged. On the one hand, Paul would be deeply troubled by the casual attitudes and high divorce rates among professing Christians in our day. How might we reverse this dreary trend and regain a zealous commitment for marital reconciliation? On the other hand, Paul's delicate balance between radical demand ("no divorce") and realistic concession ("but if you do") challenges those who would transform pastoral counsel into canon law and vote to declare divorce the unforgivable sin.

## Improvising on a Theme (7:12–16)

With verse 12, Paul turns to address "the rest," namely, Corinthian believers married to unbelievers. Early evangelism could lead to household conversion (1 Cor. 1:16; 16:15; Acts 10:2; 11:14; 16:15, 31; 18:8), but the gospel could just as easily produce household division (Matt. 10:21, 34–37; Luke 12:51–53; 14:26). And because a "good" marriage, for the typical Roman male, was one that enhanced his social status, he would have good reason to scorn a wife who had joined what looked to him like "a bizarre sect of people venerating a crucified criminal" (Hays, 122).

Evidently some members of the Corinthian church wanted freedom from such worldly allegiances. "Surely," they would argue, "the believer is defiled by sexual contact with the pagan spouse. Surely a Christian must break off intimate attachment with an unbeliever who lives in the realm of darkness and lawlessness" (Hays, 121). Mixed marriages would have been particularly awkward for Christian women, whether Jewish or Roman, whose nonbelieving husbands enjoyed supreme authority over their households (cf. 1 Peter 3:1–2).

"In taking this stance, Paul rejects the assumption—an assumption congenial to his own pharisaic background—that the pure person is defiled by contact with the unclean."—Hays, *First Corinthians,* Interpretation, 121.

Paul himself weighs in on this one. Because Jesus never addressed a "mixed" scenario, Paul felt free to offer his own apostolic counsel, like a master musician carefully completing the score of a symphony whose final pages have been lost. The basic melody line of Paul's pastoral improvisation comes in verses 12–13, where he instructs husbands, and then wives, not to initiate divorce with an unbeliever who agrees to continue the relationship. Verse 14 offers two good reasons to stay in the union: to "sanctify" the pagan partner and to preserve the children as "holy." What exactly Paul had in mind here is a bit of a puzzle. In light of verse 16, Paul can't be saying that my salvation (which he sometimes calls "sanctification") is automatically extended to my nearest kin. More likely, Paul is responding to the Corinthians on their own terms: they thought the believing partner could contract defilement; Paul counters that the nonbelieving partner could contract holiness. As Hays explains, "this extraordinary affirmation declares the power of God to work through the believer to claim and transform the spouse and children" (Hays, 121; cf. 1 Peter 3:1–2).

"[Paul] sees Christianity as a world-transforming, not merely a world-denying religion."—Witherington, *Paul's Narrative Thought World,* 321.

In the midst of this refrain, verse 15 sounds a countermelody: "but if the unbeliever chooses to leave, then let the separation take place" (NJB). This is no fuzzy appeal to "mutual incompatibility" or "irreconcilable differences." Rather, Paul foresees instances of desertion or abandonment by the nonbelieving partner, in which case, Paul adds, the believing spouse "is not bound" (v. 15). This probably means he or she is not bound to the marriage, but maybe they were simply not bound to observe Paul's previous admonitions (vv. 12–14). Either way, Paul does not ask the believing spouse to prevent the termination of the marriage. (Our distinction between legal separation and divorce was unknown in Paul's day.)

Was this freedom from marriage simultaneously freedom to remarry someone else? Paul doesn't say, probably because his Corinthian readers wanted *out* of an old union, not back *into* a new one. Like Jesus before him, Paul would roundly condemn any divorce that was obtained for the purpose of remarriage. (Such schemes were as familiar then as they are today.) Nevertheless, divorce in the ancient world invariably entailed the freedom to remarry, as Paul himself seems to imply elsewhere (7:27–28, 39; Rom. 7:1–3). Paul could have used verse 15 to issue a categorical prohibition of remarriage after desertion, but he didn't.

**Want to Know More?**

**About Paul's view of sexuality?** See Robert Jewett, *Paul the Apostle to America: Cultural Trends and Pauline Scholarship* (Louisville, Ky.: Westminster John Knox Press, 1994), 45–58.

**About asceticism?** See McBrien, *The HarperCollins Encyclopedia of Catholicism*, 100.

## Adjusting for the Long Haul (7:17–40)

The Corinthians' obsession with avoiding marital sex, or with escaping marriage altogether, meant their focus was all wrong. Paul agrees: singleness is preferable, but only for those who have the grace to make it work. Paul knows: there will be broken relationships, but married couples should strive to remain together, in marriages that are fully sexual. So far, so good. But when we come to Paul's fundamental convictions, the guiding principles upholding all this pastoral advice, some of us may be more reluctant to go along.

| 7:17 | 7:20 | 7:24 |
|---|---|---|
| To each one<br>as the Lord has assigned, | | |
| each one<br>as God has called, | Each one in the calling<br>in which he was called, | Each one in [that in]<br>which he was called<br>brothers [and sisters] |
| thus let each one live. | in this let him remain. | in this let him remain with God. |

In verses 17–24, Paul states and restates a principle we might paraphrase as "maintain the status quo." We have seen this principle at work (7:8, 10–12); now we see it clearly spelled out three times (7:17, 20, 24). The striking similarities between them appear when we keep to a rather literal rendering (see table on page 40).

Paul's intent is not to idealize or romanticize the status quo, as though the Christian should cherish all human relationships and institutions, even abusive ones, as they are. The point is, rather, that the sorts of identity markers, role distinctions, and status indicators so important to the Corinthians (and to us) have now been "rendered meaningless in light of the gospel" (Hays, 123; cf. 7:19, 22; Gal. 3:28). How prepared are we to embrace this way of thinking? What would change if we grounded our personal identity in our Christian "calling" rather than in our gender, our relationships, our social stature, our ethnic heritage, our education, our professional achievements, or our possessions?

With verses 25–38 (which Hays, 126, entitles "Counsel for Engaged Couples"), we encounter a second principle that may be even more foundational to Paul's thinking: time is short. In Paul's words, "the time has been shortened, so that from now on those who have wives should be as though they had none" (7:29, NASV). In the same breath Paul instructs those who buy to behave as though they did not possess (v. 30). Rather cryptic advice, this. Sounds like a page out of the *Heaven's Gate* new-members manual.

Paul's logic does not become clear until the end of verse 31: "because this world as we know it is passing away" (NJB). Paul lived in eager anticipation of the Lord's return and of divine deliverance from the coming wrath (1:7, 18; 15:51–52; Rom. 8:23; 13:11–12; Phil. 3:20; 4:5; 1 Thess. 1:10; 4:13–18; 5:9; cf. 2 Peter 3:10–13). Along with most early Christians, Paul firmly believed that the last days had finally arrived (cf. Acts 2:16–17; 1 Tim. 4:1; 2 Tim. 3:1; 1 Peter 4:7; 2 Peter 3:3; 1 John 2:17–18; Jude 18); that the death and resurrection of Jesus had ushered in "the ends of the ages" (1 Cor. 10:11); that the people of God were standing on the fault line been the old age and the new. In this light, Paul relegates marriage, along with wealth and possessions (v. 30), to an era that was all but passé (cf. Luke 20:34–36). There is much to do and precious little time, so Christians must weigh carefully any decision—to marry, to buy, to invest, to become enmeshed in the cares of this world.

How can we today maintain Paul's perspective on things terrestrial? Certainly not by divorcing our spouses, selling our property, and moving to an estate in California. Rather, it will be by soberly and watchfully fulfilling our responsibilities in *this* world with one eye trained on the *next.* Luke Johnson points us in the right direction:

> Christians must live as people both engaged with and detached from worldly structures. They cannot flee them, but neither can they treat them as though they were permanent or ultimate. They are to live within them "as though not" (7:29–31), a difficult feat for anyone, and particularly for people attracted to simple solutions. (Johnson, 280)

There remains, however, one rather glaring problem: the time *wasn't* short. We've been standing on this eschatological fault line for quite a while now, and the ground hasn't moved. It was Paul, not "the world as we know it," who passed away. Perhaps this means we should revisit Paul's "last days" teaching on marriage and divorce and make some adjustments for the long haul. As Hays observes, "this chapter, perhaps more than any other in the New Testament, actively *invites* us into the process of rethinking and moral deliberation" (Hays, 133). Would Paul counsel any differently if he were writing today? Would he be more hesitant to urge widows and virgins to stay single if he knew how many generations would come and go before the end of the age? (See 1 Tim. 5:14 for signs of a shifting perspective.) Would Paul be more inclined to give marriage equal billing with celibacy or even consider it advantageous for the majority of us? Would he tearfully allow women to divorce husbands whose chronic abuse extends over years, even decades? Paul described himself as one who "by the Lord's mercy is trustworthy" (7:25, NRSV) but he also saw his own counsel on these matters as cautious improvisations on the teaching of Jesus (7:12, 25–26; cf. vv. 6, 7, 17, 28–29, 32, 35, 40). The question is whether *we* are trustworthy enough to offer similarly cautious "improvisations" on Paul. This much is clear: the need for godly, spiritual discernment on matters of sex and marriage, divorce and remarriage will be with us until—well, until the last day.

"Though he may have once extolled to the Corinthians the advantages of celibacy, Paul is determined to resist this imposition of a single standard on all members of the community. He argues for options. There is more than one way to live a holy life."—Bassler, *Women's Bible Commentary,* 416.

## Questions for Reflection

1. This passage might raise questions about the authority of scripture. What do individuals do when the Bible supports a view that differs from their own on an issue?
2. Paul is offering advice on issues of marriage and divorce. Offering advice can be a delicate matter. What are some principles to follow when giving and receiving advice? Does Paul follow those principles? Why or why not? What are some examples from this passage that support your view?
3. This passage speaks to several debates in contemporary society—about the relative merits of marriage and celibacy, the proper time for sexual abstinence, and the legitimate grounds for divorce. When, if ever, is it fitting to subordinate personal convictions on such matters to the standards of the larger Christian community?
4. If you believed as Paul did that your time was short, how would that affect your attitudes? your behavior? What urgencies might you feel?

# 5 1 Corinthians 8:1–13

## Not Causing Others to Stumble

Mr. Toad simply plopped himself down on the roadway, entranced, staring fixedly after the rapidly disappearing motorcar. Moments ago he had been strolling along beside the horse cart, a few steps behind Mole, engaging Water Rat in small talk. But then, almost without warning, clouds of dust and wind blew past the little group, sending them all sprawling, spooking the old gray horse and dumping the cart into the ditch.

> "Glorious, stirring sight!" murmured Toad. . . . "The poetry of motion! The *real* way to travel! The *only* way to travel!" . . . "And to think I never *knew*!" went on the Toad in a dreamy monotone. "All those wasted years that lie behind me, I never knew, never even *dreamt*! But *now*—but now that I know, now that I fully realize! O what a flowery track lies spread before me, henceforth! What dust-clouds shall spring up behind me as I speed on my reckless way! What carts I shall fling carelessly into the ditch in the wake of my magnificent onset!" (Grahame, 36)

From that day forth, Mr. Toad was a toad possessed—firmly seized by his new "knowledge"; completely captivated by the sheer speed, the raw power, and the prestige of the automobile. On the very next morning, Mr. Toad made his way to Town and "ordered a large and very expensive motorcar" for himself (Grahame, 39). Almost immediately he was driving everywhere and crashing everywhere—seven cars and seven smashups. As Water Rat would say, he was "hopelessly incapable" behind the wheel.

So completely did this new "knowledge" consume Mr. Toad, body and soul, that when three friends (Mole, Rat, and Badger) finally tried to rein him in, he shrewdly eluded their grasp (by feigning sickness and escaping through a window). Making his way to an inn (The Red Lion), he stole a patron's car and headed for the open country, transformed (at least in his own mind) into "Toad the terror, the traffic-queller, the Lord of the lone trail, before whom all must give way or be smitten into nothingness and everlasting night" (Grahame, 113).

Unfortunately, toads are not the only ones to be captivated by new-found "knowledge," knowledge that was "never even dreamt" before. Anyone who gains new insight—into the automobile, the skateboard, or the heart of God—will face the temptation to become snooty, self-absorbed, and irresponsible. Mr. Toad could speak for many of us: "What dust-clouds shall spring up behind me as I speed on my reckless way!"

Back in Corinth, recent converts from paganism were no less susceptible to the charms and dangers of knowledge. Their intellectual discovery, their knowledge, had to do with the folly of idolatry. And this new knowledge brought them freedom and power, as it did Mr. Toad behind the wheel, but it also made them reckless. They began "driving" wildly, exploring where their new knowledge might lead, all the while oblivious to the deadly dangers posed to themselves and others. As we will see, Paul's challenge in this chapter is to show them the hazards and peril of their rambunctious ways—before it is too late!

## Scarecrows in a Cucumber Field (8:1–6)

Back in chapter 7, we recall, Paul announced he was turning to matters raised by them in their letter. First up was sex and marriage. Now he moves on to a new topic, "food offered to idols," a topic that occupies Paul (more or less) for the next three chapters. As with chapter 7, chapter 8 begins with what is probably a direct citation from the Corinthians themselves. (Note how the NRSV editors have added quotation marks; cf. NEB.) You rightly point out, says Paul, that "all of us possess knowledge" (Greek: *gnosis*). Those wondering what it is everyone supposedly "knows" must wait until verse 4 for Paul to resume his train of thought. In the meantime, Paul delivers a sober warning: "Knowledge puffs up, but love builds up" (NIV, NRSV). Knowledge by itself, unchecked and unbridled, can be

> "Idol meat was a hot-button issue in Corinth because it dramatized three much larger concerns: the problem of boundaries between church and pagan culture, the strained relationship between different social classes in the community, and the relation between knowledge and love as the foundation of the church's life."—Hays, *First Corinthians*, Interpretation, 135.

downright dangerous. Not only can it inflate the one "in the know" (4:6, 18–19; 5:2), but, in the words of Mr. Toad, it can fling many others "carelessly into the ditch" (8:11).

Verse 2 pops the bubble of those in Corinth who proudly "claim to know something." They are puffy with pride; they are smug with presumption; they claim to belong among the intellectual elite. But their knowledge is flawed, Paul says; "they do not yet know as they should." Several chapters later Paul will render this same idea into poetry, still best heard in King James English: "though I . . . understand all mysteries, and all knowledge; . . . and have not charity, I am nothing" (13:2, KJV).

Alert readers of these first two verses know exactly what to expect in verse 3. Without reading ahead we can almost hear Paul saying something like "anyone who truly *loves* others is the one who truly *knows* something." But this is precisely what Paul does not say. His thought moves in a surprisingly different direction: "anyone who loves God is known by him" (NRSV). Even more fundamental, apparently, than our love for one another is our love for God. (Can the two ever be separated?) And underlying *our* love for God, Paul contends, is *God's* "knowledge" of us. With this idea we arrive very near to the heart of Paul's thought. As Hays remarks, "the initiative in salvation comes from God, not from us. It is God who loves first, God who elects us and delivers us from the power of sin and death. Therefore what counts is not so much our knowledge of God as God's knowledge of us. That is the syntax of salvation" (Hays, 138; cf. Gal. 4:9). The church is not an academic guild whose members gain special privileges by displaying intellectual prowess; the church is a community of needy sinners who have responded to the outstretched arms of God.

**The temples of other gods and idols were very familiar to the Corinthians.**

With verse 4, Paul gets his argument back on track. Right you are, he agrees, "no idol in the world really exists," and "there is no God but one" (8:4, NRSV). Once again, these remarks may be excerpts from their letter to Paul, but they would also capture the sentiment of most first-century Jews and Jewish Christians, not least card-carrying, Torah-thumping, heresy-hunting Pharisees like Paul.

As a matter of fact, the last line of verse 4 sounds very much like Israel's cherished and often repeated *Shema:* "Hear, O Israel! The LORD is our God, the LORD is one" (Deut. 6:4, NASV).

Of course, no one would deny the physical existence of idols; pagan shrines, statues, and temples cluttered the Corinthian landscape. Rather, as Paul explains in verse 5, the claim was that those countless "so-called" deities, the gods and lords of ancient Greece and Rome, were counterfeits—fakes—pseudo-gods who lived and reigned only in the minds of their worshipers (8:5). Perhaps we should imagine a chorus of amens from Israel's Old Testament prophets, for whom exposing the myths behind pagan worship was often a full-time job. Who could forget Elijah's taunt to the drained but determined prophets of Baal?

> "Cry aloud! Surely he is a god; either he is meditating, or he has wandered away, or he is on a journey, or perhaps he is asleep and must be awakened." (1 Kings 18:27, NRSV)

Isaiah's oracles were equally barbed:

> Half of it he burns in the fire; over this half he roasts meat, eats it and is satisfied. He also warms himself and says, "Ah, I am warm, I can feel the fire!" The rest of it he makes into a god, his idol, bows down to it and worships it; he prays to it and says, "Save me, for you are my god!" (Isa. 44:16–17, NRSV)

Not to be outdone was Jeremiah:

> Their idols are like scarecrows in a cucumber field, and they cannot speak; they have to be carried, for they cannot walk. (Jer. 10:5, NRSV)

By Paul's day, Jewish monotheism had become a "fighting doctrine," a hill on which many Jews were prepared to die—quite literally (as we read in 1 Maccabees 1–2).

"But as for us," Paul continues, we know "there is but one God, the Father . . . and one Lord, Jesus Christ" (8:6). Corinthian heads nod vigorously, and so should ours. But before we nod our way into the next verse, we should pause to consider this one more closely. In a Greek Bible, more so than in English, the two lines of this verse are tight and symmetrical, looking something like this:

One God, the Father, from whom [are] all things and we for him,
and
one Lord, Jesus Christ, through whom [are] all things and we through him.

The rhythmic, even poetic pattern here has persuaded many that these words are drawn from an early Christian creed or hymn. If so, we are peering back behind Paul to witness an even older church in the very act of worship!

> "For the Hellenists, this necessarily dethroned Zeus/Jupiter as the father of the gods and father of the world. They faced the alternative of worshiping either Zeus or the Father of Jesus Christ."—Becker, *Paul: Apostle to the Gentiles,* 108.

But whether Paul was "composer" or simply "publisher," alert Jewish readers would be struck by the way these "lyrics" borrow language from Israel's scriptures. It looks like someone has taken a classic Old Testament statement about the "*LORD* our *God*" (Deut. 6:4) and transformed it into a pair of statements, about *God* the Father and the *Lord* Jesus. Notice how it works:

| ***Deuteronomy 6:4*** | ***1 Corinthians 8:6*** |
|---|---|
| The LORD is our *God,* | One *God,* the Father,<br>from whom [are] all things and we for him, |
| the *LORD* is one! | one *Lord,* Jesus Christ,<br>through whom [are] all things and we through him. |

Something remarkable is going on here. For starters, even though Paul speaks here of *both* one God *and* one Lord, he is most emphatically not conceding anything to polytheism. As N. T. Wright explains, when Paul "put Jesus and God in the same bracket he was not intending to add a second god to the pantheon" (Wright, 65). And yet this verse does seem to be redefining what we mean by "God." At the very moment the early Christians are stubbornly refusing to abandon Jewish monotheism, they are taking "the extraordinarily bold step of identifying 'the Lord Jesus' with 'the Lord' acclaimed in the *Shema*" (Hays, 140). Paul is engaged here, in other words, in a daring and dangerous high-wire maneuver, endeavoring to reinterpret Israel's sacred traditions without falling headlong into heresy.

Somehow the Christian church, over the years, has never quite climbed down from that high wire. Nor can it. It must balance precariously, in its teachings about God, about Christ, about salvation, between the twin dangers of bland respectability and utter foolishness. As G. K. Chesterton saw it:

> The Church went in specifically for dangerous ideas; she was a lion tamer. The idea of birth through the Holy Spirit, of the death of a

> divine being . . . are ideas which, any one can see, need but a touch to turn them into something blasphemous or ferocious. . . . This is the thrilling romance of Orthodoxy. . . . There never was anything so perilous or so exciting as orthodoxy. (Chesterton, 100)

We may well wonder whether Paul ever sorted out precisely *how* the paradox worked—how Christians could worship the Messiah without being guilty of idolatry. There is, however, no need to wonder about *why* Paul lays all this out right here. According to verse 6, God's people, including those in Corinth, exist "for" God, not for themselves. And they come to God "through" Christ, not on their own merits (cf. Col. 1:15–20; 1 Tim. 2:5–6). Whatever else this means, surely it must place God's purposes ahead of ours. Individual believers must never behave, in the spirit of Mr. Toad, as "lords of the lone trail, before whom all must give way or be smitten."

## Annoy or Destroy? (8:7–13)

Verse 7 is the watershed of the chapter, where Paul parts company with those glibly chanting slogans like "we all have knowledge" and "no God but One." The fact is, says Paul, that this "knowledge" about God and idols (8:4, 6) is not shared deep down by every believer. Many in the Corinthian church were fresh converts out of paganism. They had frequented the local temples all of their lives, sharing in cultic meals and paying tribute to the Roman pantheon. The mere fact that they were now worshipers of the one true God did not mean they would instantly feel at home in God's world, any more than an emancipated slave or released prisoner adjusts overnight to his newfound freedom. A number of these young converts had what Paul calls a "weak conscience." Richard Hays explains:

> "In *public* sacrifice, . . . after the requisite symbolic amount of meat had been burned and after the priests had received their share, the rest of the meat fell to the magistrates and others. What they did not need, they sold to the shops and markets; and therefore, even when meat was bought in shops, it might well have been already offered to some idol."—Barclay, *The Letters to the Corinthians,* 72.

> Some members of the fledgling church are so accustomed to thinking of the idols as real that they cannot eat the idol meat without conjur-

ing up the whole symbolic world of idol worship; they are dragged back into that world and so "defiled." (Hays, 141)

Verses 8 and 9 belong together. It is true, Paul agrees, that "food will not bring us close to God" (8:8, NRSV). Eating brings no spiritual advantages, and abstaining carries no stigma. But just because food itself is neutral (1 Cor. 10:25–26; Rom. 14:2, 6, 14; Mark 7:19; Acts 10:15), believers dare not pretend that their personal eating habits have no effect on others. "Take care that this liberty of yours does not somehow become a stumbling block to the weak" (8:9, NRSV). By stubbornly insisting on your "right" (Greek: *exousia;* authority, ability, freedom) to eat idol meat, you are provoking a major crisis for your "weaker" brothers and sisters.

Verse 10 throws wide open a window on ancient Corinth, showing what all this might look like in real life. It helps if we remember that pagan temples in the ancient world were multipurpose structures. Not only were they centers for ritual sacrifices and cultic meals, but the temple precincts also had to serve as the first-century equivalent of the modern restaurant, union hall, and community center. The wealthier Corinthians (including some members of the young church) would be expected to attend any number of social functions at the local temple, and, invariably, the menu would include ritually sacrificed meat. Not to partake would be awkward, perhaps even insulting to the host.

Let's say you've accepted an invitation to some festivity at the temple, Paul writes. While you are dining, another believer—one with a "weak" conscience—picks you out of the crowd. He doesn't "know" what you know; he doesn't have the "freedom" that you have. Don't you see how your behavior could "bolster" him (Greek: *oikodomeo,* build up; "strengthen" NASV; "embolden" NEB) to follow your example and eat idol meat in violation of the standards of his conscience? Your "freedom" would be causing him to "fall" back into the idolatrous world from which he has only recently been delivered! (Notice how different is Paul's advice, in 10:23–33, regarding ritually sacrificed meat that is sold in the market and consumed in the home.)

"Paul is willing to forego not only the specific practice of eating idol food but also the eating of meat altogether if that is necessary to protect the weak from stumbling. The effect of this policy, of course, is that it places Paul himself de facto among the ranks of the weak."—Hays, *First Corinthians,* Interpretation, 142.

In the final verses of the chapter, Paul reiterates no fewer than five times the potentially ruinous effect of dining in pagan temples:

| | |
|---|---|
| 11 | "the one who is weak is *destroyed* by your knowledge" |
| 12 | "[you are] *sinning* against those brothers and sisters" |
| 12 | "[you are] *wounding* their weak conscience" |
| 12 | "[you are] *sinning* against Christ" |
| 13 | "[eating food could] *cause* my brother or sister to *stumble*" |

It is tempting to tone down the rhetoric of verse 11. Did Paul honestly think a church member might perish, might be spiritually lost, if he or she adopted a high-risk behavior already being practiced by another believer? Apparently, yes. As Paul goes on to say in chapter 10, there is no such thing as "safe" idolatry. "You cannot partake of the table of the Lord and the table of demons" (10:21, NRSV; cf. 10:7, 11–14, 20, 22). Gentile Christians drawn back into pagan idolatry were no less susceptible than was ancient Israel to divine wrath.

Even more stunning perhaps is the announcement at the end of verse 12 that to "wound" these weak ones is to sin against Christ. Jesus' parable of the Last Judgment comes to mind: "just as you did not [feed, clothe, or visit] one of the least of these, you did not do it to me" (Matt 25:45, NRSV; cf. 10:40–42). It is hard to imagine a more forceful way of declaring Christ's spiritual unity with his people and his intense concern to protect the vulnerable among them.

Unfortunately, a little word in verse 13 has generated more than its share of confusion in recent years. According to the King James Version, Paul says "if meat *make* my brother *to offend*, I will eat no flesh while the world standeth, lest I *make* my brother *to offend*." In Shakespeare's day, "offend" was a solid translation of the Greek *skandalizo*, a verb meaning something like "cause to stumble" or "cause to sin" (see NRSV, NJB, NIV, NASV, etc.). For Paul, the mere thought of dragging a brother or sister down into sinful behavior was more than enough reason to abstain from meat of any kind.

> "[Paul] states the first great principle, that liberty must be limited by love."—Erdman, *1 Corinthians*, 89.

The problem is that for most of us today "offend" means something rather different—something like "displease," "annoy," or even "disgust." Clearly, Paul did not write this chapter to discourage Christians from annoying one another.

> The concern is not that the weak will be *offended* by the actions of the *gnosis-boasters;* Paul's concern is, rather, that they will become alienated from Christ and fall away from the sphere of God's saving power, being sucked back into their former way of life. (Hays, 142)

The lesson here is *not* that a self-appointed committee of the most narrow-minded and intolerant members of the church should screen all disputed activities. Paul's urgent appeal must not be reduced simply to a warrant for prohibiting activities some deem "offensive," like dancing, body piercing, or the use of alcohol. Rather, Paul's message targets those in the church who have "knowledge" (vv. 1–6) and an accompanying inner "freedom" (v. 9) to engage in certain disputed behaviors (vv. 9–10). Should not the one who "knows" demonstrate the greatest restraint and sensitivity in the presence of an impressionable brother who could join in, but only by violating the standards of his own conscience?

When we read this chapter closely with chapter 10 (vv. 14–22), we will also find ourselves challenged to identify which cultural practices and social networks we should abandon as incompatible with our allegiance to Christ. In some regions of the world (e.g., Korea or Malaysia), where each home has a family altar and where food is regularly presented to ancestral spirits, Paul's warnings may seem as current as yesterday's headlines. But even in secular North America, Christians can be found "unwittingly eating in the temples of the idols that surround us" (Hays, 143). Some of us pay homage at the shrine of material wealth or worldly fame or political influence. Others venerate the god of personal comfort or physical beauty or national pride. Still others display single-minded devotion to the pursuit of "extreme" experiences. But whether we worship at a family altar, a bank account, or a mirror, whether we bow before the flag or the opinion poll, scripture challenges each of us to consider how our earthly allegiances undermine the exclusive Lordship of Jesus Christ and threaten to harm those for whom he died.

### Want to Know More?

**About Gnosticism, Stoicism, and other philosophies?** See Roetzel, *The Letters of Paul,* 19–36.

**About other gods in ancient times?** See Robert M. Grant, *Gods and the One God,* Library of Early Christianity (Philadelphia: Westminster Press, 1986), 19–71.

## Questions for Reflection

1. Verse 3 of this passage refers to being "known by God." What does it mean to be known by God? If God created us, wouldn't God know us? What other scriptures can you think of that refer to God's knowing us?
2. What is Paul saying when he speaks of the existence of other gods and other lords (v. 5)? Do they exist or not? Paul seems to assume that they do. Do you agree or disagree with Paul's assumptions? Why?
3. In this unit, Paul asks the Corinthians to oblige the weaker ones. In Unit 3, Paul admonished them to stay away from anyone who was openly engaged in immoral behavior (1 Corinthians 5). How can we distinguish between the weak and the sinful among us?
4. According to the writer of this study, scripture challenges us to consider how earthly allegiances might undermine the Lordship of Christ. What are those things to which you give allegiance? What if your answer includes family, job, and the pursuit of education? Are they bad things? Why or why not?

# 6 1 Corinthians 9:14–27

## *All for the Sake of the Gospel*

"This pearl has become my soul," said Kino. "If I give it up I shall lose my soul." A common fisherman from a long line of common fishermen, Kino lived with his wife Juana and baby Coyotito in a small brush-house by the Gulf. Kino was common, but his pearl was not. They called it "the Pearl of the World." His people had dreamt about it, they sang about it, and now Kino was the one to find it. And all the village found it with him, and all the villagers followed him and his family to the pearl buyers, and they watched as the buyers offered Kino a mere 1,000 pesos, and they wondered as Kino's face became hard as he pushed his way back through the crowd and returned home.

That day the world changed forever for Kino. He began to fear. First he feared losing the pearl, and then he feared the night and those who came by night to steal it from him. And then he feared the strangers and the strange places he would encounter with Juana on their long and treacherous journey to "that monster of strangeness they called the capital," where he would sell his pearl to buy happiness for his family.

> It lay over the water and through the mountains, over a thousand miles, and every strange terrible mile was frightening. But Kino had lost his old world and he must clamber on to a new one. For his dream of the future was real and never to be destroyed, and he had said "I will go," and that made a real thing too. To determine to go and to say it was to be halfway there. (Steinbeck, 69)

Kino was right to be afraid. Thieves attacked him in the night. They tried to kill him and to steal his pearl. They torched his home and forced him and his family to flee. But Kino was undaunted, for his treasure had come to possess him, to enslave him, to compel him to embark on a dangerous quest to find someone, anyone, who would take his pearl and offer in return a fair price. Little did he know the price he himself would have to pay.

> "He lives with a powerful sense of obligation to God, defined now by his relationship to Christ."—Hays, *First Corinthians,* Interpretation, 154.

Compulsion is a powerful force. To be "under compulsion" is no longer to be in control. It is to be constrained, coerced, overpowered. Such is the plight of Paul as we encounter him in 1 Corinthians 9. By his own admission, he is constrained and compelled by the gospel of Jesus Christ. Like Kino, Paul had found his "pearl." In fact, the day Paul laid hold of the gospel—or rather, the day it laid hold of him (cf. Gal. 1:15–17; Phil. 3:12)—he also "lost his old world" and had to "clamber on to a new one." And Paul's discovery thrust him out too, on a quest filled with risks and haunted by enemies. But as we will see, the force that drove Paul did not spring from within him, nor should it be compared to Kino's iron will and blind determination. How then should we understand the force that drove the apostle Paul?

## Fire in the Bones (9:14–18)

The first part of chapter 9 is Paul's skillful defense of his right to get paid for being a church-planting, Bible-teaching, risk-taking missionary. After all, he is an apostle (vv. 1–2) who deserves the same kind of care as the likes of Cephas (= Peter; vv. 3–6). Common sense confirms the principle (v. 7); scripture commands it (vv. 8–10); and Jewish priests illustrate it on a daily basis (v. 13). And if that's not enough, the point is spelled out explicitly in verse 11: because Paul has "sown spiritual good" among the Corinthians, he should be free to "reap . . . material benefits" from them (NRSV).

The clincher of his pay-the-preacher argument comes in verse 14: "In the same way, the Lord commanded that those who proclaim the gospel should get their living by the gospel" (NRSV). Paul believes that Jesus himself endorsed this principle during his own sojourn on earth. Although these words were penned well before our four Gospels came along, Paul is probably alluding to Jesus' instructions to the seventy—to those he sent out in pairs ahead of him: "Remain in the same house, eating and drinking whatever they provide, for the laborer deserves to be paid" (Luke 10:7; cf. 1 Tim. 5:17–18).

Why didn't Paul quote Jesus in the first place? Why withhold the best wine until the end of the feast? Hays points out that though Paul "saved his knockdown argument for last, yet he introduces it without fanfare or elaboration, allowing the point to carry its own considerable weight" (Hays, 152). Perhaps the greatest payoff is the way this sets up such a powerful contrast with verse 15, the pivot verse of the whole chapter: "But I have made no use of any one of these rights"—not even the one granted by Christ himself!

Paul has argued at length for his "right" (Greek: *exousia;* cf. 9:4, 5, 6, 12, 18) to draw material support from his spiritual dependents. Now, however, he just as emphatically refuses to exploit that right (cf. 9:12). Paul is so animated, in fact, that his grammar can't keep up with his passion. He tosses one sentence aside unfinished only to start on another: "It would be better for me to die than . . . No one will make my boast an empty one!" (9:15b). (Unfortunately, most English versions tend to "fix" what is broken here, which means some of Paul's intensity is muted.)

But what "boast" does Paul want to protect? Does he simply want to be known as Paul-the-preacher-who-won't-pass-the-plate? A very different impression of the apostle emerges if we continue into the next three verses. Verse 16 declares that preaching the gospel was Paul's calling, his destiny: "I am under compulsion; for woe is me if I do not preach the gospel!" (NASV). Like Jeremiah the prophet, God's message burned like a fire in Paul's bones (Jer. 20:9; cf. 4:19; 23:9). Like Kino the fisherman, Paul could not abandon the treasure thrust into his hands; to proclaim the gospel had become his very life. As Gordon Fee explains:

> To preach the gospel of Christ is *not something he chose to do* . . . it is *something he must do.* God had ordained such a destiny for him from birth and had revealed it to him in the event of the Damascus road (Gal. 1:15–16). From that time on, proclaiming Christ to the Gentiles was both his calling and his compulsion. (Fee, 418)

So Paul had come to accept his "destiny," to submit to the divine "force." But unlike Luke Skywalker, Paul was not called to engage in cosmic combat nor to defeat singlehandedly the forces of evil. Rather, his calling was to proclaim the good news that evil had already been defeated on the cross!

Despite appearances, verse 17 does not really set forth two live options for Paul. The point is not that on good days, Paul *freely chooses* to obey, but that on other occasions he only *grudgingly* fulfills his duties. Even on the best of days, Paul is no more a volunteer than was any common slave in the Roman Empire. In Paul's own words, "I am simply discharging a trust" (NEB). Slaves take home no paycheck. Servants do not listen for applause (cf. 4:1–5; Luke 17:7–10).

According to verse 18, Paul's "pay" is to preach without "payment." His "boast" is his freedom to offer salvation with no strings attached. Paul has every right to expect missionary support, but he chooses instead to live off his earnings as a leather worker (cf. 1 Cor. 4:12; Acts 18:3). As both Hays and Fee suggest, Paul's ministry was a dramatic enactment of the gospel itself. Paul's "renunciation of rights allows him to share in the pattern of Christ's own sacrificial action and thereby paradoxically to share in the lifegiving blessings of God" (Hays, 153).

Many Christian ministers know firsthand how money sometimes gets in the way. In many rural communities and even in some extended families, the pastor will always struggle for respect until he gets a "real" job—preferably one that gets the hands dirty or one that generates some marketable commodity. But as for the rest of the congregation, as well as for so-called tentmaker missionaries who provide their own support, none can accuse them of sponging off the church or of using the gospel to get rich. In a world driven by profit margins and economic self-interest, those who reach out to the poor or who offer good news to the weary, with no possibility of personal gain, provide irresistible confirmation of their message.

**Want to Know More?**

**About Paul and the Law?** See C. K. Barrett, *Paul: An Introduction to His Thought* (Louisville, Ky.: Westminster John Knox Press, 1994), 74–87.

**About slavery?** See Hawthorne, Martin, and Reid, *Dictionary of Paul and His Letters*, 881–83.

## One Demotion after Another (9:19–23)

It's easy to see a thread weaving through the next five verses; the two ends dangle from verses 19 and 22 (NRSV):

| | |
|---|---|
| 9:19 | "I have made myself a slave to all, so that I might win more of them." |
| 9:22b | "I have become all things to all people, that I might by all means save some." |

Paul is unveiling his missionary strategy here. We have seen how carefully he has avoided becoming entangled in patronage and in obligations to supporters. Now, however, we learn that he freely adapts his behavior to fit in among those he wants to win. Paul sees himself as a slave to Christ (7:22; Eph. 6:6); he works out that slavery by "submitting himself in various ways to the cultural structures and limitations of the people he hopes to reach with the gospel" (Hays, 153).

Verses 19–22a provide four illustrations of Paul's voluntary enslavement. The first three belong together, and they prepare the way for the fourth. The following table not only highlights the fourfold symmetry, but it also tries to preserve the form of Paul's Greek.

| *Paul's Context* | *Paul's Response* | *Paul's Purpose* |
|---|---|---|
| To the Jews | I became as a Jew | that I might win Jews. |
| To those under the law | [I became] as under the law (not being myself under law) | that I might win those under law. |
| To those without law | [I became] as one without law (not being without God's law but "inlawed" to Christ) | that I might win those without the law. |
| To the weak | I became weak | that I might win the weak. |

I offer several comments. First, the opening pair of examples obviously overlaps. To be a "Jew" is to be "under the law" of Moses. Paul was both. Or was he? His language here shows how radically his perspective has changed since becoming a follower of Jesus. Hays senses the irony: "To relate to Jews as a fellow Jew (cf. Acts 21:17–26) is for Paul now seen as an act of accommodation!" (Hays, 153). Even Paul's most valued possession, his ethnic heritage as a son of Abraham and a child of the covenant, pales in the light of his allegiance to Christ. (Do we esteem *our* earthly ties as lightly?)

Second, Paul twice feels the need to qualify his remarks. (See the parentheses in the middle column above.) In verse 20, Paul says he "became [that is, he behaved, he chose to live] as though under the law." But then he hastily adds, "though I myself am not under the law" (NRSV). And in verse 21, Paul "became as one without the law," to which he adds, "though I am not free from God's law but am under Christ's law" (NRSV). Paul wants his readers to understand why he sometimes adopts the mealtime behavior of kosher Jews, when at other times he can relax Jewish standards (especially concerning food laws and circumcision) and fit in nicely among Gentiles. On the one hand, Paul is no longer answerable to the covenant of Moses; the reign of "the law" has now passed (Gal. 3:23–4:7). On the other hand, being "law-free" does not mean being "lawless"; Paul has not jettisoned all moral restraint. Rather, "he is asserting that the pattern of Christ's self-sacrificial death on a cross has now become the normative pattern for his own existence" (Hays, 154; cf. 1 Cor. 11:1; 2 Cor. 4:10–12; Gal. 2:19–20; Phil. 2:5–8; 3:10–11). (Does the pattern of Christ's self-sacrificial death govern our lives?)

**_To Eat or Not to Eat?_**

Though Paul may not have been bothered by meat offered to idols, there were some who might be drawn back into the pagan rites. How hard it is to forget! "The danger is the emotional connection between one's past and present."—Peter Richardson, *Paul's Ethic of Freedom* (Philadelphia: Westminster Press, 1979), 128.

Finally, the last illustration (v. 22) is most likely the focal point of the passage. Paul has "become" weak for the sake of the "weak" among the Corinthians. On the heels of chapter 8, these "weak" must include those (in Corinth and elsewhere) who could not eat idol meat with a clear conscience (cf. 8:13). More broadly, it refers to the lower classes—those who had to work for a living and who were vulnerable to the oppression and the hostilities of the rich. Isn't this the story of Paul's life? As a self-supported, often-afflicted, much-maligned, itinerant missionary to the Gentiles, Paul's career was essentially one demotion after another; his calling was to "become weak" for the sake of the gospel (9:12, 23; cf. 2:1–5; 4:9–13; 2 Cor. 4:7–18; 11:16–33; 12:7–10). (Are we as committed to downward mobility?)

"One of our greatest necessities is to learn the art of getting alongside people; and the trouble so often is that we do not even try."—Barclay, *The Letters to the Corinthians*, 84.

In all this, Paul's goal was to "save some" (v. 22) and, eventually, to "share with them" in salvation's blessings (v. 23). In Paul's mind, salvation was not only something that unfolded in the *present* (1:18); it was also something scheduled to arrive in the *future* (Phil. 3:9–21). The genuine risk that some followers might not "share" those future blessings occupies Paul in the next four verses where he puts the finishing touches on his argument.

## Aerobics-for-Jesus (9:24–27)

Some ten miles east of Corinth was the site of the Isthmian games, a biennial spectacle second only to the Olympics in reputation.

Because Paul himself was in Corinth roughly between 49 and 51 C.E., archaeologist Oscar Broneer suggests that the apostle may have made his way to the games of 51. There he could witness events like boxing, wrestling, track, and discus, and would have numerous opportunities to preach to the crowds. But even if Paul never set foot in that stadium, the imagery in these verses would obviously resonate with his earliest readers.

The emperor, too, might wear a wreath.

If it is true that "the runners all compete, but only one receives the prize" (v. 24, NRSV), then Christians should run to win. It is easy for those of us who have grown up in a culture that embraces macho, in-your-face, win-at-all-costs athleticism to miss Paul's point, which has nothing to do with individual achievement and competitiveness, and everything to do with caring for the needs of others. As Hays aptly notes, "If Paul had known about team sports, they would have given him a richer metaphor to make his point: team players must couple rigorous training with restraint of individual egos for the sake of the team's success" (Hays, 158).

What does it take to win? According to verse 25, it takes "self-control." All participants in the games had to prepare rigorously, apparently for a minimum of ten months. For all their efforts, Paul adds ironically, the victor receives a "perishable wreath." Granted, along with the wreath came prestige and popularity (though probably not commercial endorsements), but the "crown" (Greek: *stephanos*) itself would soon disintegrate and be discarded.

How much more, then, should Christians train and strive for the "imperishable" prize that awaits? The crown Paul describes is not some achievement award for distinguished saints—the heavenly equivalent of a Most Valuable Player trophy. It is, rather, the reward of salvation itself. To attain the prize of heaven, Paul says, "I punish my body and enslave it" (v. 27, NRSV). We arrive, once again, at comments easily misconstrued. Paul is not advocating self-flagellation, as though true spirituality consists of denying bodily appetites and desires. Nor does it mean Paul would endorse the modern aerobics-for-Jesus movement. Paul knew all about the cuts and scrapes that come with manual labor, as well as the painful blows inflicted by hostile opponents (cf. Acts 14:19–22; 16:19–24; 18:1–18; 20:1–3). But his talk of bodily bruises is really code for the self-restraint that believers must demonstrate toward one another. Again, Hays captures the point:

> The self-control to which Paul is calling the "strong" is precisely the discipline of giving up their privileges *for the sake of others in the community.* They are to exercise self-discipline by giving up their rights to certain foods—and perhaps some of their privileged social status as well. This is a minor consideration, Paul suggests, in contrast to the prize set before us. (Hays, 156)

Paul's ascetic comments seek to benefit the larger community, to "build up the body of Christ" (Eph. 4:12–17). Otherwise, self-denial just sets one apart. In the words of Kathleen Norris: "If one engages in a severe discipline—an extreme diet, or daily work-out, or all-encompassing hobby—strictly for oneself, for the purposes of self-improvement, then that is all it is. It may even disconnect us from others, taking up so much time and energy as to weaken our commitments to family and friends."—Kathleen Norris, *Amazing Grace: A Vocabulary of Faith* (New York: Riverhead Books, 1998), 365.

At the end of verse 27 Paul envisions a disturbing scenario. Apparently even he, a preaching apostle, could be "disqualified" from the race if he fails to exercise self-control (cf. 1 Cor. 3:17; 10:12, 21–22). Although Paul was not plagued by the nagging fear he might lose his salvation (cf. Rom. 8:28–39; Phil. 1:23), he did contend that believers (himself included) must persevere (1 Cor. 15:1–2; Rom. 11:22; Col. 1:21–23; 2 Tim. 4:7–8). To define a Christian exclusively in terms of an initial "profession" of faith without regard for subsequent faithfulness would be incomprehensible to Paul.

"Any spiritual discipline can be manipulated for our own ends rather than offered as a means of God's transforming grace in us."—Marjorie J. Thompson, *Soul Feast: An Invitation to the Christian Spiritual Life* (Louisville, Ky.: Westminster John Knox Press, 1995), 144.

So the Paul of 1 Corinthians 9 is a driven man. Not driven to succeed or to outdo the competition, but driven nonetheless. He was a man under compulsion whose every move was measured to advance the gospel. In sharp contrast to Kino, the pearl fisherman, Paul was not driven to retain ownership of his treasure, to cling to it with all his might. Nor was he bent on selling it for a profit. On the contrary, Paul's driving passion was to give his pearl away, freely and without charge: "I am under compulsion; for woe is me if I do not preach the gospel!" (NASV).

How would *we* behave differently if we were less concerned about our own careers and more compelled by the cause of Christ?

## ? Questions for Reflection

1. The writer of this unit draws on an illustration from John Steinbeck. In that illustration, he uses the phrase "that day the world changed forever for Kino." What are some of the things in your life that "changed forever"? Why?
2. Paul refers elsewhere to "the weak." Using a concordance, look up some of those references. What does Paul mean by "weak" or "weaker"?
3. Both here and elsewhere in the letter, Paul alludes to the teachings of Jesus. Almost certainly, the first letter to the Corinthians was written before any of the Gospels as we have them. What do you think were the sources for Paul's information about Jesus? That is, how did Paul know what Jesus said?
4. Paul concludes this chapter with an athletic metaphor. Even today, athletes have a very high profile in our culture. Think about the attention given to athletics today. Do athletes typically exemplify the "downward mobility" described in this unit? Why or why not?

# 1 Corinthians 11:17–34 — 7

## *This Is My Body*

It was fashioned in the days of Uther Pendragon, father of King Arthur and Overlord of all Britain. Shaped like a large ring and furnished with seats enough for fifty, it would come to be known far and wide as the "Round Table." According to Merlin the Wise, a wondrous magic held sway over that Table. "Whenever a worthy knight appeared, then his name appeared in letters of gold upon that seat that appertained unto him; and when that knight died, then would his name suddenly vanish from that seat which he had aforetime occupied" (Pyle, 143).

Perhaps the legend of how this enchanted Table came into the hands of Arthur of Camelot, and of how he first assembled the Knights of the Round Table, deserves a study guide of its own. As the story goes, the evil Duke, Mordaunt of North Umber, is seeking the hand of the beautiful maiden, Lady Guinevere. The Duke challenges the Lady's father and almost wins his bride when, at the last possible moment, a White Knight appears in front of the castle—King Arthur in disguise. He overthrows the Duke and, in due course, wins the love of the Lady Guinevere.

So it was that Guinevere's father bestowed the enchanted Round Table upon King Arthur. It was a wedding gift, a dowry, which meant the Round Table was established in Camelot on the very day King Arthur and the Lady Guinevere were wed. That day, King Arthur's name magically appeared in gold letters on the back of the Seat Royal, as did the names of thirty-two other knights on the backs of thirty-two other chairs. Having taken their places at the Round Table, they rose together and swore an oath, a covenant of knighthood:

> that they would be gentle unto the weak; that they would be courageous unto the strong; that they would be terrible unto the wicked and the evil-doer; that they would defend the helpless who should call upon them for aid. (Pyle, 154)

Then, as if to seal and unite that wondrous fellowship, the Knights of the Round Table shared their first meal together:

> Each knight brake bread from the golden paten, and quaffed wine from the golden chalice that stood before him, giving thanks unto God for that which he ate and drank. (Pyle, 154)

Nothing would ever be the same. To be sure, each man would retain his own name and title—like King Pellinore and Sir Gawaine. Each would engage in his own heroic conquests and die his own noble death. But from that day forward, those knights would be remembered above all else for their place among "The Ancient and Honorable Companions of the Round Table."

The legend of Arthur and his Table may remind us of another king and another table. Jesus invited his earliest followers to dine with him—to break bread and drink wine at the table of his fellowship. And some of them would turn out to be heroic warriors as well (or, at least, fearless missionaries) who accomplished deeds chivalrous, noble, and praiseworthy. But wherever they roamed and whatever their stories, their true home would always be around a table, sharing bread and drinking wine with one another, in the presence of their king.

So much for a charming medieval analogy that might, for a week or two, elevate the way we think about Christian communion. But perhaps there is more here than fantasy and nostalgia. As we will see, the earliest readers of First Corinthians may well have felt more comfortable dining with King Arthur than with the Lord Jesus. For Arthur's Table was a closed circle, with a limited number of much-coveted places. To be included among the "Honorable Companions" of the king, one had to be of noble birth, of proven character, and of established worth. One also had to be male. A seat at the Round Table was a guarantee of prestige and worldly influence, an unequivocal statement about status, power, and social hierarchy.

Not so around the Lord's Table. Admittance to that circle is open to any and all who have pledged their loyalty to the king: not just knights in shining armor but also weary and tarnished peasants; not just men but women and children as well; not just the tested and true but also the weak, the unstable, and the unworthy. In direct contrast to the way Arthur ran Camelot, those invited to the Lord's Table are called to relinquish worldly titles and claims to distinction. No wearing crowns during meals.

As Paul discovered, this kind of thinking and behaving was entirely foreign to many in the Corinthian congregation, especially to those few who could boast "of noble birth" (1:26, NRSV), whom we might call the "knights" of the church. Those young believers in Corinth, and all believers ever since, would have to learn that those who flaunt human titles and display personal wealth at the Lord's Table bolster the very discord and divisions Christ's death was intended to overcome.

## The Trouble with Normal (11:17–22)

Paul seemed cheery enough back in verse 2, but with verse 17 the mood shifts rather suddenly, like storm clouds on the prairies: "Now in the following instructions I do not commend you, because when you come together it is not for the better but for the worse" (NRSV). You'd be better off, Paul jeers, to stay in bed or maybe take in a play—anything but go to church! Equally stormy is verse 22: "What! Do you not have homes to eat and drink in? . . . What should I say to you? Should I commend you? In this matter I do not commend you!" (NRSV). Even if we allow for a little Pauline hyperbole, the indignation behind these words is hard to miss.

The term for "come together" can also mean "be united." "Paul's rebuke to the Corinthians plays off this double sense of the term: when they come together as a church they paradoxically do not 'come together' in unity and peace."—Hays, *First Corinthians,* 194.

The reason for Paul's outrage has to do with, of all things, table manners—with the way the Corinthians were eating together. From the very beginning, Christians assembled in groups to eat a common meal (typically in the home of one of the wealthier church members; cf. Rom. 16:5, 23) and to share together the bread and the wine of communion (cf. Acts 2:46). Although this practice was rooted in the Last Supper of Jesus and his disciples, as Paul reminds us in verses 23–25 (cf. Luke 22:14–22), the combination of food and fellowship was common throughout the Mediterranean world. At Passover, Jewish families ate lamb and bread together, and drank wine, to recall their deliverance from Egypt (Exodus 12). And the monks who kept the

Dead Sea Scrolls regarded their communal meals so highly that novices had to serve two full years' probation before they were welcome at the table. As for pagan meals, archaeologists can show us ancient invitations to sacred temple dinners in honor of gods like Serapis and Demeter (cf. 1 Cor. 10:20–21). And we need only read Plutarch's *Table Talk* to get a sense of the richness of mealtime conversation.

So the problem was not that communal meals were a novelty—on the contrary. Precisely because they were so common, and because Roman society had already defined what was "normal" and respectable mealtime behavior, the Corinthian believers naturally assumed those "norms" would apply also in the church—which brings us to verse 21, where Paul complains that "each of you goes ahead with your own supper" (NRSV). Many have suggested these words target the early birds who couldn't wait to begin eating (cf. NIV, NEB, NLT). In which case, verse 33 instructs these ones to be patient: "wait for one another" (NRSV). But Paul's reference to church "schisms" in verse 18 and to "those who have nothing" in verse 22 suggests that the problem in Corinth was not simply one of timing. Rather, the wealthier church members were hoarding their own choice fare and refusing to share with those who came, apparently later, with little or nothing in hand.

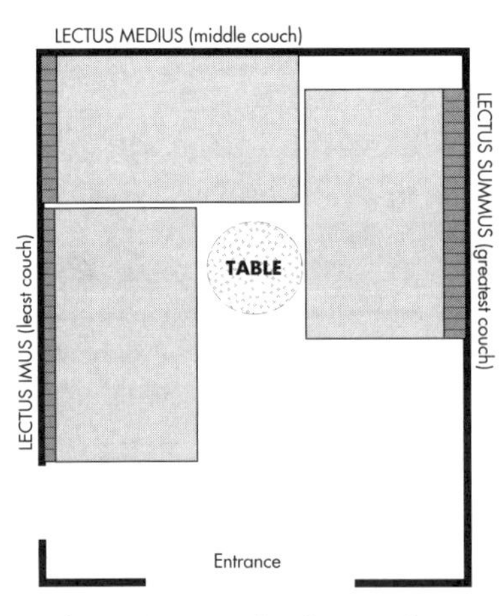


**Meal participants reclined on couches.**

If such a blatant display of selfishness seems incredible to those of us raised on church basement potlucks (where even the children get plenty of everything), we must remember how "normal" it was for the Roman upper classes to flaunt their wealth at the expense of the poor. It was all part of the social game. We must picture a scene in which a prosperous church member—perhaps a public official or successful merchant—arrives at the home of an equally well-to-do friend for the evening meal. He is ushered into the dining chamber and invited to recline on one of, say, nine couches (two or three guests per couch), his location chosen carefully to correspond to his social ranking. Slaves serve up generous portions of the best food and drink, and things are well underway before the poorer, working-class believers arrive to join the bustling house-church meeting. Their place is the atrium, an outer room where they must sit or stand, hoping to benefit from the generosity, or at least the left-overs, of their richer brothers and sisters.

Much about this class-conscious state of affairs may remind us of the modern world of air travel. First-class passengers board the plane at their leisure (often earlier than the rest) and occupy spacious quarters shielded from the teeming masses of the economy class. Rumor has it they also enjoy superior cuisine, unlimited beverages, and their own staff of doting attendants. But these parallels are tenuous at best. Most passengers who feel twinges of jealousy (as they peel the lids off of their plastic juice containers) have no idea what it was like for the poor in Roman Corinth—the slaves, artisans, and day laborers—who went "hungry" (v. 21) and were "humiliated" (v. 22) while their brothers and sisters in Christ consumed more than their share. But here is where Paul may surprise us. The offense he finds most grievous is not their mere disregard for the poor, nor is it the tendency of some toward gluttony or drunkenness (v. 21). Paul is most outraged because the highhanded selfishness of the rich makes a mockery of the Lord's Supper (v. 20) and shows disdain for "the church of God" (v. 22), all of which brings us to a very familiar set of verses.

## Mingling Memory and Hope (11:23–26)

Right here in the midst of a vigorous challenge to the richer members of the church, Paul takes time to tell a story—*the* story about Jesus' final supper with his disciples. He had no Gospel of Matthew, Mark, or Luke to turn to; what he had instead were the remembered sayings of Jesus and the treasured traditions about his life. Verse 23 says Paul "received" these treasures and was "handing them on." That's how it worked in those early years. We must think of Christianity, in its infancy, less as a philosophy or moral code than as a narrative. As Hays observes:

> The telling of the story of Jesus' death and resurrection stood at the center of Christian proclamation from the beginning. Paul is not giving the Corinthians new information here; rather, he is recalling to mind the story that he told them about the foundational redemptive event; a story that they themselves repeat—or *should* repeat—every time they gather at table. (Hays, 197–98)

The Jesus story Paul tells happened "on the night he was handed over" (11:23). According to most versions (NRSV, NASV, NEB, NLT,

NJB, NIV, etc.), this refers to Judas' act of betrayal in the garden of Gethsemane (Luke 22:48). But why would the earliest Christians have used that treacherous act as their historical landmark for the Lord's Supper? Was it, perhaps, to provide a humbling reminder that the burden of Jesus' death lay in part upon his own followers? The alternative is to understand "he was handed over" as a statement not about Judas' dirty deed but about *God's* handing Jesus over to death. This fits well with Paul's language elsewhere (Rom. 4:25; 8:32) and also with the words of Isaiah 53:6, 12 (according to the Greek version).

"Parents may feel something similar when they take their son or daughter to kindergarten the first day, or to college, and 'hand them over' to people they don't even know and just leave the child there. . . . Such was the risk of the Incarnation, God handing [an] infant son to us."—H. Stephen Shoemaker, *GodStories: New Narratives from Sacred Texts* (Valley Forge: Judson Press, 1998), 277.

On that very night, Paul recalls, Jesus "took a loaf of bread, and when he had given thanks, he broke it" (11:23–24, NRSV). Then, near the end of the meal, Jesus "took the cup also" (11:25). Simple gestures, these—repeated daily in every Jewish household and every year at Passover. But on this occasion these simple gestures came with some remarkable commentary—words that have echoed loudly down through the history of the church. The fact that these remarks also appear in three of the four Gospels indicates that they were repeated often, and treasured, from the very beginning.

**The Bread**

| | |
|---|---|
| 1 Cor. 11:24 | "*This is my body* that is for you. Do this in remembrance of me.* |
| Matt. 26:26 | "Take, eat; *this is my body.*" |
| Mark 14:22 | "Take; *this is my body.*" |
| Luke 22:19 | "*This is my body,* which is given for you. Do this in remembrance of me." |

**The Cup**

| | |
|---|---|
| 1 Cor. 11:25 | "This cup is the new *covenant* in my *blood.* Do this, as often as you drink it, in remembrance of me." |
| Matt. 26:27 | "Drink from it, all of you; for this is my *blood* of the *covenant,* which is poured out for many for the forgiveness of sins." |
| Mark 14:24 | "This is my *blood* of the *covenant,* which is poured out for many." |
| Luke 22:20 | "This cup that is poured out for you is the new *covenant* in my *blood.*" |

Evidently, no writer provides a pure transcript that would satisfy the modern obsession with verbatim reportage. Nevertheless, the substantial overlap confirms that Paul wasn't just making all this up; Jesus really did consider this Last Supper to be profoundly symbolic of his mission and of his imminent death. Especially striking are the similarities between Paul and Luke. In both versions Jesus' body is (given) "for you" (echoing Isa. 53:12), and both have Jesus establishing a "new" covenant (invoking Jer. 31:31; cf. 2 Cor. 3:6; Heb. 8:8).

Down through the years, the church has thought (and fought) hard about the words "this is my body" and "this is my blood." But whatever those expressions meant to Jesus and his earliest followers, when Paul tells the story he places the greatest weight elsewhere—on the phrase "in remembrance of me." Like Passover, which was a "day of remembrance" for Israel (Ex. 12:14), the Lord's Supper is a dramatic reminder of what God has done to deliver a new Israel through the death of Christ. This must be what Paul means when he says, in verse 26, "you proclaim the Lord's death." As Hays explains, "the community's sharing in the broken bread and the outpoured wine is itself an act of proclamation, an enacted parable that figures forth the death of Jesus 'for us' and the community's common participation in the benefits of that death" (Hays, 199–200).

The final three words of verse 26 should not be overlooked: "you proclaim the Lord's death *until he comes*" (NRSV). The bread and the cup do more than reenact the past; they also preview the future. But once again, this idea is not original to Paul; according to the Gospels, Jesus promised to eat again with his disciples in the coming kingdom (Matt. 26:29; Mark 14:25; Luke 22:18; cf. Matt. 8:11; 22:10). So, Paul says, the Lord's Supper is what Jesus' disciples do while they wait for that future to arrive. "The meal acknowledges the *absence* of the Lord," Hays explains, "and mingles memory and hope, recalling his death and awaiting his coming again" (Hays, 199).

## Magic Working Backward (11:27–34)

With this final paragraph we discover why Paul opted to retell the story of the Last Supper. It was clearly not to supply the Corinthians with new information—verse 23 suggests Paul was repeating himself—but rather to change their behavior. "Therefore," Paul says in verse 27, it matters very much what happens when you eat together. Once you know The Story and allow it truly to become *your* story, you will no longer be able to treat each other as you do.

> "To eat unworthily means to eat in a way that provokes divisions, with contemptuous disregard for the needs of others in the community."—Hays, *First Corinthians*, Interpretation, 200.

Regrettably, Paul's idea of eating and drinking "in an unworthy manner" (v. 27) has often been misunderstood, as has his call for believers to "examine" themselves (v. 28). This is not a summons to intense personal introspection as a warmup to Holy Communion. Nor is Paul proposing that believers grovel in self-contempt, nor that they purge every sin before they can be worthy to approach the Table. Paul's concern here is not for greater *self-awareness* but for more *self-forgetfulness.* Uncle Screwtape, the fictional devil who must help his nephew Wormwood waylay a young Christian (see Unit 1), puts it this way:

> Keep his mind on the inner life. He thinks his conversion is something *inside* him and his attention is therefore chiefly turned at present to the states of his own mind. . . . Encourage this. Keep his mind off the most elementary duties by directing it to the most advanced and spiritual ones. Aggravate that most useful human characteristic, the horror and neglect of the obvious. (Lewis, *Screwtape,* Letter III, page 16)

For all their self-professed advancement and spirituality (1:7; 3:1, 18; 5:2), the wealthier Christians in Corinth were neglecting something extremely "obvious"—the urgent need to set aside their own interests and begin caring for the needs of the poor among them. They ate "unworthily" when they erected social barriers and promoted divisions in the church between the haves and the have-nots.

Something serious is at stake here. In verse 27 Paul warns the culprits that they may be guilty or liable for the "the body and the blood of the Lord." Contrary to much Christian tradition, this is not an indictment of those who have a "low" view of the sacraments (however well-deserved that indictment may be). The point is, rather, that when believers profane the Lord's Table by mistreating each other, they "repeat the sort of sin that made the death of Christ necessary" (Hays, 201). If the Table represents above all else God's radical grace and Christ's selfless love, then those who dine together around it are called to extend that grace and that love to others.

Verses 29–32 insist that some among them have already incurred divine judgment, in the form of sickness or even death (v. 30), for failing to "*judge* the body" (v. 29). At least two questions arise. First, what are we to make of the notion that physical maladies in the Christian community may be directly related to behavior around the Table? However improbable or superstitious this may seem to some of us, we must first hear these words from within Israel's prophetic tradition. Deuteronomy 27–29, for example, testified that those who violated the covenant would suffer curses and death. And prophets like Isaiah (1:10–17) and Amos (2:6–8; 7:4–10) directed scathing rebukes toward Israel for embracing a form of religion that enslaved the poor. Who are we to suggest that God's passion to defend the weak and to punish their oppressors has mellowed over time?

But second, Paul calls believers to "judge the body" (v. 29). The Greek word behind "judge" (*diakrino*) is a bit of a puzzle, as a quick glance at our English versions reveals (NRSV, NEB: *discern;* NJB, NIV: *recognize;* NLT: *honor;* NASV: *judge*). But we must also choose between at least four different "bodies": (1) Jesus' physical body, (2) the Lord's body as represented in the bread, (3) each believer's own body, or (4) the body of Christ, that is, the church. Is this a call to focus our thoughts during the meal upon Christ's broken body on the cross, upon that "sacred head now wounded"? Or might this be a reminder about the sacramental character of the Eucharist?

**Want to Know More?**

**About meals?** See Osiek and Balch, *Families in the New Testament World,* 193–214.

**About the development of the New Testament?** See John Barton, *How the Bible Came to Be* (Louisville, Ky.: Westminster John Knox Press, 1997).

**About the Lord's Supper?** See Markus Barth, *Rediscovering the Lord's Supper* (Atlanta: John Knox Press, 1988).

Faced with such quandaries, the nod should always go to the reading that makes best sense *in the context.* That context, including Paul's opening sally (vv. 17–22) and parting shot (vv. 33–34), clearly shows a sustained preoccupation with the self-centered behavior of the church's richer members. With that in mind, "judging" or "discerning the body" must mean, in Hays's words, "recognizing the community of believers for what it really is: the one body of Christ" (Hays, 200). The best commentary on this verse may come from Paul himself: "Because there is one bread, *we who are many are one body,* for we all partake of the one bread" (1 Cor. 10:17, NRSV; cf. 12:12–26). The church, in all its grisly complexity and bewildering diversity, is *one* because of the broken body of Jesus. So when that church gathers around the Table, her *oneness* should be so palpable you can almost taste it. A eucharistic prayer from the second century echoes Paul's cry for unity: "As this broken bread was scattered upon the mountains, but was brought together and became one, so let thy Church be gathered together from the ends of the earth into thy kingdom" (*The Didache* 9:4).

"The next time you walk down the street, take a good look at every face you pass and in your mind say *Christ died for thee.* That girl. That slob. That phony. That crook. That saint . . . *Christ* died for thee. Take and eat this in remembrance that Christ died for *thee.*"—Frederick Buechner, *Wishful Thinking: A Theological ABC* (New York: Harper & Row, 1973), 53.

Granted, church would be much more civilized and the Lord's Table far more dignified if we limited participation to society's elite, to the blue bloods, the luminaries. Perhaps we should screen church members for economic background and social standing, and interview candidates before admitting them to the Table. Perhaps, like King Arthur, we should have limited seating and provide engraved nameplates for the few who measure up. By these standards, Paul's vision for Christian community is much less comfortable, less predictable, less civilized. But it is also a much more faithful expression of the unity—not the humanly contrived homogeneity—that Christ died to establish. The magic of the Round Table worked to *exclude* the unworthy and to *separate* noble knight from common serf. But the far deeper "magic" of the Lord's Table works precisely backward: not to *exclude* but to *include* the unworthy; not to *divide* but to *bring together* nobles and peasants, rich and poor, young and old, into the one community we call the church.

## ? Questions for Reflection

1. Some might refer to the topic of this passage as "Dinner Etiquette," but it is specifically addressing the wrongful practices of some in the Corinthian church during the Lord's Supper. What were those wrongful practices? Why would Paul speak against those practices?
2. Is the practice of the Lord's Supper a time of remembering back or a time of looking ahead? Why?
3. Verses 29–30 speak about a harsh punishment for those who participate in the Supper in an unworthy manner. How do you respond to Paul's warning that those who eat in an unworthy manner will be punished, especially for inappropriately taking the Supper?

4. Hays states that we should recognize "the community of believers for what it is; the one body of Christ." What does it mean to be the one *body* of Christ? What does it mean to be the *one* body of Christ?

# 8 1 Corinthians 12:1–31

## *Concerning Spiritual Gifts*

Picture a community in which everyone fits perfectly into the social network, in which each member delights in performing the task for which he or she has been specially prepared. Picture a society of individuals entirely comfortable with their own strengths and weaknesses, with their own abilities and limitations. No selfishness, no jealousy, no competition. Pure utopia. A vibrant, healthy "body" made up of many happily interdependent members.

You've just pictured Aldous Huxley's *Brave New World,* a futuristic society where babies aren't born; they're "decanted" from bottles in factories controlled by Predestinators and Directors of Hatcheries. It's a world where children are conditioned in their sleep to embrace a predetermined social caste, however high or low it might be. Let's listen in on the message some of the more gifted children would hear night after night:

> "Alpha children wear grey. They work much harder than we do, because they're so frightfully clever. I'm really awfully glad I'm a Beta, because I don't work so hard. And then we are much better than the Gammas and Deltas. Gammas are stupid. They all wear green, and Delta children wear khaki. Oh no, I *don't* want to play with Delta children. And Epsilons are still worse. They're too stupid to be able to read or write. Besides they wear black, which is such a beastly colour. I'm *so* glad I'm a Beta." (Huxley, 18)

In Huxley's hypnotized, mechanized society, Henry Ford is Lord. (The story takes place, after all, in the seventh century "After Ford.") Much like employees in an automobile factory, everyone knows what he or she must do to keep the line moving. And not only do they *know* it, they've been conditioned to *like* it; as the Director puts it, the secret to happiness is "liking what you've *got* to do" (Huxley, 10). No independent thinking here. No personal agenda. Just social cooperation, behavioral conditioning, and perhaps, at the end of the day, *soma,* the drug of choice.

*Brave New World* starkly presents us with two options: we can pursue the blissful but robotic utopia of a socially engineered, totalitarian state or we can opt for the discordant chaos of a society that insists on protecting personal freedom. It's a choice, as Huxley himself put it, "between insanity on the one hand and lunacy on the other" (Huxley, viii). Little did he know, back in 1932, how soon the world would have to choose between the two.

Control versus chaos. Structure versus spontaneity. Can a community hold together and yet celebrate genuine, rough-and-tumble diversity? Does it become a mere machine if individual members are not free to rebel? The stunning thing about the church of Paul's imagination, as opposed to the bland community Aldous Huxley foresees, is the way it maintains such a delicate balance between form and freedom. Apparently no one told Paul he had to choose between the two; he wants both. So his challenge to the Christian community in 1 Corinthians 12 is to celebrate and encourage the wildly diverse contributions of each individual. At the same time, however, he challenges each individual to use his or her gifts in ways that strengthen and support the corporate assembly. This is neither behavioral manipulation (à la Huxley) nor a drug-induced passivity. In Paul's vision, when the Spirit empowers believers, they become "freely bound"—creatively committed to the needs and interests of one another, and to the dynamic unity of the church.

## Badge of Spirituality or Mark of Grace? (12:1–11)

As Paul takes up the topic of spiritual gifts, we should probably imagine him once again composing his thoughts in response to a letter from Corinth (cf. 7:1, 25; 8:1), a letter that has not survived (no doubt to the Corinthians' great relief). Paul announces he does not want the church to be "ignorant." This is Paul's way of assuring his readers that the following advice about "spiritual things" (Greek: *pneumatika*) is entirely trustworthy (cf. 10:1). Most English versions (e.g., NRSV, NIV, NEB, KJV, NASV, NJB) refer here to "spiritual gifts," but the word "gifts" (Greek: *charismata*) does not actually occur until verse 4. The difference is subtle, but may be significant, for, as we will see, the Corinthians were inclined to exult in the ways—especially the flashy, dramatic ways—the Spirit was working among them. So Paul cautiously reminds them that their spiritual inheritance is, above all, an expression of God's grace (Greek: *charis*); whatever we call them, the gifts of the Spirit are not an achievement award or badge of *spirit*-uality.

"The trouble is that they are treating these manifestations of the Spirit as signs of their own spiritual sophistication and power."—Hays, *First Corinthians,* Interpretation, 208.

With verse 2 Paul recalls once again (cf. 8:7) the pagan, idolatrous past of many in the church. Before their conversion to Christ, life was a matter of being "enticed and led astray to idols that could not speak" (NRSV). In that former predicament, some had no doubt experienced pagan forms of "ecstatic" or "inspired" speech. However close were those pagan encounters of the spiritual kind, verse 3 provides a fail-proof test for discerning the empowering presence of God's Spirit: "no one can say 'Jesus is Lord' except by the Holy Spirit" (NRSV). In other words, "only where the lordship of Jesus is authentically confessed can we know that the Holy Spirit is at work" (Hays, 208).

An incidental comment in verse 2 reveals how closely Paul associates the followers of Jesus with the Old Testament people of God. According to most versions, Paul refers to a time now past when the Corinthians were "pagans." This word (Greek: *ethne*) is actually the standard term for "Gentiles" (cf. KJV). In other words, as Hays explains, "Paul is unmistakably suggesting that they have turned away from idols to serve the living God of Israel (cf. 1 Thess. 1:9) and thereby become grafted into Israel (cf. Rom. 11:17–24)" (Hays, 209).

Verses 4–6 lay out, in a triple, we might even say "trinitarian," formula the central principle Paul yearns to get across—that behind the lavish abundance of spiritual gifts stands one Giver:

| | |
|---|---|
| there are varieties of gifts (*charismata*) | but the same Spirit (*pneuma*) |
| there are varieties of services (*diakoniai*) | but the same Lord (*kyrios*) |
| there are varieties of activities (*energemata*) | but the same God (*theos*) who activates (*energon*) all of them in everyone |

It is tempting to overinterpret a passage like this—to squeeze from it more than it was intended to convey. For example, the association of the *Spirit,* the *Lord* (Jesus), and *God* in these verses is striking, though it does not require that Paul held to a fully developed doctrine of the

Trinity such as emerged in later centuries. (In the third century, for example, Dionysius of Rome would speak of "the Divine Triad" [Bettenson, 32].) Nevertheless, it would be fair to say that Paul's Spirit/Lord/God language here—the earliest of its kind in the New Testament—has "clear Trinitarian implications" (Fee, 588).

Likewise, Paul probably did not mean to distinguish between three distinct classes of divine creativity: gifts, services, and activities. We may just as well roll all three ideas into one: God graciously gives us "gifts" to be used "in God's strength" to "serve" one another. Paul's main goal here is to sharpen the contrast between the diversity "down here" and the unity "up there," not to offer technical definitions or to specify who gives what.

Verses 7 and 11 reiterate the key idea of our chapter:

| | |
|---|---|
| 7 | TO EACH ONE is given the manifestation of THE SPIRIT for the common good. |
| 11 | All these are activated by one and THE same SPIRIT, who allots TO EACH ONE individually just as the Spirit chooses. |

If verse 7 underlines how broadly gifts are distributed, verse 11 stresses how they all derive from a single Spirit-source. And both verses remind us that gifts are not given according to *human* merit, choice, or natural ability, but wholly according to *divine* freedom (cf. 12:18; perhaps in response to prayers: 12:31; 14:1, 13), and further that each believer will be gifted in some way, in order to benefit the community (cf. Rom. 12:3–8; Acts 2:17–18).

"There are parts of the body which are never seen but whose function is more important than any other; there are those who serve the Church in ways that win no publicity, but without whose service the Church could not go on."—Barclay, *The Letters to the Corinthians*, 116.

In between these two bookends, verses 8–10 contain a list of spiritual gifts—the first of several such lists in Paul's letters (cf. 12:28, 29–30; 13:1–3, 8; 14:26; Rom. 12:6–8; Eph. 4:11)—designed to establish beyond all doubt the extravagant diversity of the Spirit's work in the church. Paul provides nothing like a comprehensive gift index, much to the dismay of many modern readers. Nor does he list them in a particular order, except for tongues, which is saved for last (cf. 12:28, 30). Nor does he feel compelled to mark out clear boundaries between one role and the next, like the lines between Alphas and Betas in Huxley's *Brave New World* or between official events in the Olympics. In fact, several of Paul's expressions seem to overlap (e.g., wisdom and knowledge; healings and miracles) and others go unmentioned (cf. teaching in 12:28–29; 14:6; Rom. 12:7; and Eph. 4:11; giving in 13:3 and Rom. 12:8). Notice also that some gifts appear in the plural (e.g., healings, workings of miracles, discernings of spirits, kinds of tongues), as if to suggest they were not considered permanent possessions but rather temporary endowments, distributed repeatedly as the need arose.

## Celebrate or Tolerate? (12:12–26)

Spanning the next seventeen verses is Paul's famous body analogy for the church. Long before Paul penned these words, ancient pundits recognized the human body as a handy metaphor for Greek society. Shortly before Paul's day, Roman historian Livy described how an orator named Menenius Agrippa persuaded underclass deserters to rejoin the Roman establishment. He did it by spinning a fable about a body whose hands, mouth, and teeth so resented the belly that they stopped feeding it (*Early History of Rome* 2.32). The deserters got the point. A century later, writing about the Jewish rebellion against Rome, Josephus complained that anarchy had spread from Jerusalem to the countryside, much as the limbs of the body become inflamed when an infection strikes a central member (*Jewish War* 4.406). And listen to the way Maximus of Tyre (second century) describes city life:

> The gifts are a preview of what is to come. "[The Spirit] is the power of God driving towards the end of history and carrying us forward to the destiny disclosed and anticipated in the resurrection of Jesus Christ."—Alasdair I. C. Heron, *The Holy Spirit: The Holy Spirit in the Bible, the History of Christian Thought, and Recent Theology* (Philadelphia: Westminster Press, 1983), 51.

> A city is an entity blended together by the cooperation of all. It is the same way with the body's use, which is of many kinds and requires many things, and is preserved by the joint contribution of the body's parts to the functioning of the whole: the feet carry, the eyes see, the ears hear, and so on. (Malherbe, 149)

Maximus asks what would happen if the feet "out of annoyance with the rest of the body" insisted only on rest, or if the molars "refused to pay attention to their proper work." "What would result," Maximus asks, "but the destruction of the man? That, indeed, is what happens in the political communion" (Malherbe, 150).

So we should probably excuse the Corinthians if they didn't find Paul's body metaphor particularly novel. What may have caught them off guard, however, was the way Paul put a *familiar* metaphor to work in a *new* way. As Hays explains, Paul deploys the body metaphor "not to keep the subordinates in their places but to urge more privileged members of the community to respect and value the contributions of those members who appear to be their inferiors, both in social status and in spiritual potency" (Hays, 213). We'll see this particularly clearly in verses 21–26.

Verse 12 contains a surprise ending. We might expect Paul to say: "just as the body is one and has many members, so it is with the *church*." What Paul actually says is: "so it is with *Christ*." So closely did Paul link the community of saints with their crucified and risen Lord that he could slide effortlessly between the two. It is tempting to trace this "church = Christ" idea all the way back to Paul's encounter with Jesus on the Damascus road (Acts 9:1–5; cf. 1 Cor. 8:12; 12:27).

If verse 12 declares that the church's *many* members are really *one,* then verse 13 explains how this state of affairs could come about: all of us, Paul says, have been immersed in the Spirit. The idea is probably not that the Spirit performs a baptism (cf. NIV, NASV, NLT, KJV) but that the Spirit is the domain or realm into which believers are baptized or initiated (cf. NEB, NRSV, NJB). And the purpose behind this "Spirit-baptism," this "Spirit-drink," is unity: "in the one Spirit we were all baptized *into one body*—Jews or Greeks, slaves or free" (NRSV).

> "Conversion, for Paul and the Corinthians, was an experience of the Spirit which was like the outpouring of a sudden flood or rainstorm on a parched ground, and which made their lives like a well-watered garden (Jer. 31:12)."—James D. G. Dunn, *Baptism in the Holy Spirit* (Philadelphia: Westminster Press, 1977), 131.

In Paul's imagination, the world divides rather neatly along certain lines (cf. Gal. 3:28; Col. 3:9–11). One can be a *Jew* (and heir to Israel's rich heritage) or a *Greek* (cf. 1:22; 9:20–21). Alternatively, one can be *free* from the legal claims of others, or one can be a *slave* (cf. 1:26). Elsewhere Paul distinguished between *rich* and *poor* (11:22), or between *men* and *women* (11:3; 14:34). But however we slice it, Paul's point is that *all* such distinctions—of race, class, wealth, gender—must no longer divide those who have been drawn together into the singular, Spirit-empowered body of Christ. How ironic, even tragic it is that so many quarrels have arisen over how best to live out our shared life in the Spirit!

Verses 14–19 look at the problem of disunity "from below"; that is, from the vantage point of those Corinthians who desired to *do* or to *be* something they were not. It is easy for us to imagine administrators and helpers (12:28) yearning to speak in tongues or to heal, though we should not try to interpret each image in verses 15–17 (foot, hand, sensory organs) as code for a specific gift. The point of the parable comes in verses 18–19: not only does God want diversity in the body, but God is the one who gifts each member and places each member in just the right place. "Each person," Hays concludes, "should accept gracefully and gratefully whatever gifts God has given and use them for the benefit of the community" (Hays, 215). Unlike the brainwashed, I'm-*so*-glad-I'm-a-Beta citizens of Huxley's utopia, we rarely, if ever, find contentment to be automatic.

"A conversion of the imagination will be necessary for those in a position of privilege truly to see themselves as bound together with the weaker members of the body."—Hays, *First Corinthians,* Interpretation, 220–21.

Verses 20–26 look at the same problem, but now "from above." Now the focus is on those who, because of gift or social ranking, deem others to be inferior, even unnecessary. Imagine, says verse 21, the eye looking down its nose, so to speak, at the hand. Likewise, picture the head wagging disdainfully at the lowly feet. In the church, such snooty attitudes would surely cause the weaker members "to feel despised and even ostracized from the body because they do not have the same exalted spiritual experiences" (Hays, 220).

Verses 22–24 take the body metaphor in a sharply different direction: now we are reminded that "weaker" body parts are truly indispensable (v. 22), and that "shameful" ones must be shown greater honor (v. 23). Paul's reference to "weaker" parts (the internal organs?) may be a subtle challenge to those flaunting their "knowledge" at the expense of the "weak" in the church (cf. 8:1–13; 9:22). Likewise, the "shameful" (i.e., sexual) organs probably represent the less presentable, lower-class members of the church who need to be "clothed" and "honored" by those above them. Such an appeal would make little sense in the seventh century After Ford; toward lower castes the higher ones are taught to display only cool detachment and condescension. "Gammas are stupid," after all.

According to verse 25, God wants the church to celebrate, not merely tolerate, the diversity among its members. Instead of segregation, selfishness, and schism in the body—recall the ugly scene in 11:17–34—Paul yearns for mutuality and caring interdependence.

Notice, with Richard Hays, that verse 26 "does not speak of what *should be,* but of *what is:* the body really *is* diminished and pained by the suffering of any of its members. The same principle applies also to the honor shown any one member: the body really *does* celebrate it together" (Hays, 216, emphases added).

Present-day monasteries are communities devoted to prayer and service.

Surely here, finally, we've found a point of contact between Huxley's world and Paul's, for verse 26 reads like a primitive version of the pithy maxim "when the individual feels, the community reels" (Huxley, 62). In fact, the two ideas could not be more opposite. In a Huxley-esque utopia, passionate, feeling individuals are dangerous. They destabilize the community and must be sedated with soma. In the Spirit-led communities that Paul envisions, however, each member takes up as his or her own the cares, the joys, and the woes of the other. We fulfill our calling in the church when we "rejoice with those who rejoice and weep with those who weep" (Rom. 12:15).

## Shake Your Head "No" (12:27–31)

As Paul winds up this part of his argument, he finally declares openly what he has been implying all along: "you are the body of Christ" (v. 27; cf. v. 12). As members of the church we are joined to one another because we share together the life of Christ. Sounds rather pious, perhaps even a bit mystical—that is, until we are required to sit directly beside those other body parts in church, when they "sing out of tune, or have boots that squeak, or double chins, or odd clothes" (Lewis, *Screwtape,* Letter II, page 12). Somehow our theology of the church always seems more believable in the abstract.

Then follows, in verse 28, another gift list, like the one in verses 8–10, but with a few noteworthy changes. First, Paul adds "apostles" and "teachers" (cf. 14:6, 26) as well as "helpful acts" (cf. Rom. 12:8) and "gifts of guidance" to the earlier inventory, confirming that these lists were never meant to be comprehensive and suggesting that Paul built them more or less on the fly. Here he appears to be moving away from his earlier focus on the more flashy, "miraculous" gifts so cherished in Corinth.

Second, Paul explicitly orders the first three gifts: "first apostles, second prophets, third teachers." Is this a ranking of authority? Or does it refer to a temporal sequence, in that apostles (like Paul) planted the church before others (like Apollos) came along and helped it grow (cf. 3:5–14; Eph. 2:20)? Certainly Paul viewed his apostolic calling to be authoritative and foundational (4:14–21; 9:1; 14:37; Rom. 15:15–16; Gal. 1:15–16); here (and at Eph. 4:11) he acknowledges that apostles, like every other calling or empowerment, are among God's gifts to the church.

Finally, the gift of tongues once again appears last on the list (cf. 12:10, 30). Far from being *the* mark of the Spirit, or the *greatest* gift, tongues is simply one of many ways the Spirit likes to endow the church. As verses 29–30 declare (with almost tedious repetition), no one person receives every gift, and no one gift goes out to every person. Each of Paul's seven questions follows the same rhetorical pattern: "Not all have such and such a gift, do they?" Shake your head, "No." Whenever the church is tempted to require lockstep uniformity, to elevate one gift over all the others as the believer's membership card or badge of spirituality, she must return to these verses and heed their urgent cry for diversity.

## Want to Know More?

**About gifts of the Spirit?** See Hawthorne, Martin, and Reid, *Dictionary of Paul and His Letters*, 339–47.

**About the Trinity?** See Guthrie, *Christian Doctrine*, 70–96.

**About utopian communities?** See Mark Holloway, *Heavens on Earth: Utopian Communities in America, 1680–1880* (New York: Dover Publications, 1966), and Gerald and Patricia Gutek, *Visiting Utopian Communities: A Guide to the Shakers, Moravians and Others* (Columbia: University of South Carolina Press, 1998).

Our chapter ends with a twofold preview of coming attractions. Paul first urges his Corinthian counterparts to "strive for the greater gifts." To decipher that cryptic comment, one must read on at least until 14:1–5 (cf. 14:39), where prophecy is given the nod over tongues because it is so readily intelligible and therefore so edifying in church. Then, Paul pledges to show them "a still more excellent way." The stage is set for the drama of chapter 13.

## Questions for Reflection

1. How can a community celebrate diversity and maintain unity?
2. What is the difference between a "spiritual gift" and a natural tal-

ent? Would you consider musical talent, or the ability to draw, a spiritual gift? Why or why not?

3. Verse 9 refers to the gift of faith. By definition, don't all believers have faith? Is Paul being consistent in his use of this term? Using a concordance, find other references in this letter (and in the other letters of Paul) to faith. What is the gift of faith?
4. Verse 26 speaks about suffering together and rejoicing together as members of one community. What are tangible ways that we can suffer with, or rejoice with, our Christian friends, sisters, and brothers? Do we do this? Why or why not?

# 9 1 Corinthians 13:1–13

## *Love Never Ends*

Garrison Keillor recalls, as only he can, the time his very small, very conservative, very Protestant church almost split in two. It all happened at Wednesday-night Bible study, when Brothers Louie and Mel went head to head on the issue of tongues,

> Louie arguing that this manifestation of the Spirit was to be sought earnestly, Mel holding that it was a miraculous gift given to the early Church but not given by God today. I forget the Scripture verses each of them brought forward to defend his position, but I remember the pale faces, the throat-clearing, the anguished looks, as those two voices went back and forth, straining at the bit, giving no ground—the poisoned courtesy ("I think my brother is overlooking Paul's very clear message to the Corinthians . . . ," "I think my brother needs to take a closer look, a prayerful look, at this verse in Hebrews . . .") as the sun went down. . . .
>
> "Perhaps," Grandpa offered, "it would be meet for us to pray for the Spirit to lead us," hoping to adjourn, but both Louie and Mel felt that the Spirit had led, that the Spirit had written the truth in big black letters—if only some people could see it.
>
> Bible reading finally ended when Flo went up to bed. We heard her crying in the bathroom. Al went up to comfort her. Grandpa took Louie aside in the kitchen. Mel went straight home. We all felt shaky. (Keillor, *Wobegon,* 133–34)

How often has this conflict been rehearsed, with only slight variations, down through the years? Christian brothers engage in verbal combat. Aunt Flo is reduced to tears; a young lad to confusion (soon to blossom into cynicism); everyone to feeling "shaky."

More tragic, perhaps, than the uncharitable duel itself is the fact that the territory under dispute, the point of contention, is the gracious work of God's Spirit in the church. Why does what God has given to strengthen and unite believers so often become the source of bitter, even bloody combat? What is it about spiritual gifts—those supernatural graces that enable us to rise above our petty selves and contribute in some modest way to the Christian community—that promotes so much pride, envy, resentment, self-obsession? Why does God's best tend to bring out our worst?

In this light it becomes much clearer why Paul, right here in the middle of a lengthy discourse on spiritual gifts (1 Corinthians 12–14), suddenly turns his gaze toward the virtue of love. He is reminding the Louies and the Mels of the church (and they are many), even as they "strain at the bit" to get it right, that our gifts and abilities will never amount to anything unless we also practice love.

## Poisoned Courtesy (13:1–3)

These first three verses are so wonderfully composed and elegantly arranged that any comments seem almost impertinent. We are on hallowed ground here, among some of the most cherished and recited verses in all of scripture. Without love, Paul writes, every gift, however miraculous (13:1–2), and every effort, however noble (13:3), amount to nothing. He begins this chapter where he ended the last—with the gift of tongues. "If I speak in the tongues of mortals and of angels, but do not have love, I am a noisy gong or a clanging cymbal." Although some think that "tongues of angels" is simply Paul waxing eloquent or overstating his point, it is more likely that both Paul and the Corinthians thought tongues-speech, at least some of the time, employed the language of heaven. Richard Hays (223) points us to the interesting parallel in the *Testament of Job* 48–50 (a Jewish text from roughly the same period), in which Job's three

**Brass vases could have been used to echo and resonate sounds.**

daughters, aided by specially colored cords, take to singing hymns to God in various angelic dialects.

Human or angelic, this speech was highly regarded in the town of Corinth. Yet Paul says that the speaker is nothing more than a "noisy gong" or a "clanging cymbal" without love. The "gong" may be the ancient equivalent to a megaphone or voice amplifier, but we can't be sure. Likewise, though the "cymbal" was used by pagan cults, it isn't clear whether Paul had this background in mind as he wrote. In any case, Paul's point is not in doubt: however eloquent, impressive, or miraculous my speech, if I lack love I am reduced to a "nerve wracking rattle" (Jordan, 66).

The same holds for the gift of prophecy, the ability to receive a word from the Lord for the congregation (cf. 12:10; 14:1–5). What if, Paul muses, I were a superprophet who knew "*all* mysteries" and possessed "*all* knowledge" (v. 2)? What if I were a Daniel to whom God revealed "deep and hidden things" (Dan. 2:22)? What if I were a Moses with whom God spoke "face to face" (Ex. 33:11)? Paul of course could boast of his own close encounters and insider information (1 Cor. 15:51; 2 Cor. 12:1–4; Gal. 1:12). And this sort of special knowledge was obviously highly prized in the Corinthian community as well (1:5; 8:1–13; 12:8).

Alongside various gifts of knowing Paul places the gift of believing: "and if I have all faith, so as to remove mountains." This is the God-given ability to trust God for the extraordinary (cf. 12:9; Rom. 12:3). Such faith marked the ministry of Jesus and would eventually (though not initially) characterize his disciples' lives as well (Acts 3:16; 13:11; 14:9–10; cf. Matt. 17:20; 21:21–22). Although neither Paul nor Jesus had literal "mountain moving" in mind, this sort of trust in God is no less radical. Paul delays the dramatic conclusion to all of this until the very end of the verse and then punches it out in a few short words: if I have all of this but no love, "I am nothing."

> "To give as a grim duty, to give with a certain contempt, to stand on one's own little eminence and throw scraps of charity as to a dog, to give and to accompany the giving with a smug moral lecture or a crushing rebuke, is not charity at all—it is pride, and pride is always cruel for it knows no love."—Barclay, *The Letters to the Corinthians,* 118–19.

With verse 3, Paul shifts from spiritual *gifts* to heroic *deeds*—two radical acts of self-sacrifice. What if I "give away all my possessions," Paul asks. Again we are reminded of Jesus' teachings: the rich young ruler heard Jesus say, "Go, sell your possessions, and give the money to the poor" (Matt. 19:21; cf. Luke 14:33). Here is a puzzle. Doesn't the act of spending one's last dime on the poor count for anything? Doesn't it please God to see us obeying Jesus' call for selfless generosity? Doesn't true love show itself precisely in this sort of charitable behavior? Certainly, Paul would reply, to feed the poor is a good thing. But, he would add, even our most selfless acts can fail to qualify before God when we are otherwise marked by lovelessness.

Verse 3 includes a second act of heroism that nevertheless counts for nothing apart from love: "if I hand over my body so that I may boast" (NRSV, cf. NLT). Many versions (e.g., KJV, NASV, NIV, NEB, NJB) differ sharply at this point, because a number of ancient manuscripts read *kauthesomai* ("that I may be burned") instead of *kauchesomai* ("that I may boast"). In Greek it's a difference of two letters. If Paul wrote "be burned," he obviously had in mind the most extreme form of self sacrifice (cf. Dan. 3:15–18; 2 Macc. 7:1–6; 4 Macc. 6:24–30). But the weight of evidence tilts slightly toward "boast," by which Paul probably meant he could lay down his life in order to "boast" before God on the last day (cf. 1 Cor. 9:15; 2 Cor. 1:14; 2 Tim. 4:6). Either way—boast or burn—it's a waste of time unless love is the driving force.

## Muscular Love (13:4–7)

Normally we encounter these verses somewhere between "Here Comes the Bride" and "Wedding March." We've managed to embed them, as Hays says, in a "quagmire of romantic sentimentality" from which they are rarely extricated (231). Of course this passage is well suited for any young couple entering into matrimony. But most older folks, whose marriages have weathered a storm or two, will say that this kind of robust, muscular love begins to emerge only around about the tenth anniversary. Paul's concern, in any case, was not to provide ministers with a handy text for wedding homilies, but to serve up an in-your-face challenge to the Corinthians (including all of us honorary Corinthians) for their extremely *un*loving behavior toward one another. A table of terms and passages may help us think through this densely packed cluster of verses.

> "The purpose of chapter 13 is to portray love as the sine qua non of the Christian life and to insist that love must govern the exercise of all the gifts of the Spirit."—Hays, *First Corinthians*, Interpretation, 221.

| *Phrase from NRSV* | *Paraphrases and Synonyms* | *Parallel Passages* | *Corinthian Problems* |
|---|---|---|---|
| patient | long forbearance | Rom. 2:4 (describing God); 1 Thess. 5:14 | 11:33—rich eating before poor arrive |
| kind | merciful | Rom. 2:4 (describing God); 1 Tim. 1:12–17 | |
| not envious | not jealous | 2 Cor. 12:20; Gal. 5:20 | 3:3–4—jealous rivalry and bickering over leaders |
| not boastful | does not brag, behave as a windbag, strut | 1:29–31; 3:21; 4:7; 5:6 | 5:6—self-confident boasting over sinful behavior |
| not arrogant | not puffed up or proud | 4:6, 18–19; 5:2; Col. 2:18 | 8:1—puffed up by knowledge without love |
| not rude | does not act disgracefully or shamefully | Rom. 1:27 | 11:20–22—the rich humiliating the poor |
| does not insist on its own way | does not seek its own advantage (NJB) | 10:33; Phil. 2:4; Rom. 15:1–3 | 10:24 (cf. 8:10)—eating idol meat without regard for others |
| not irritable | not provoked to wrath | Acts 15:39; 17:16 | |
| not resentful | never keeps track of evils committed | Luke 23:34; 2 Cor. 5:19 | |
| does not rejoice in wrongdoing | is not glad about injustice (NLT) | 2 Thess. 2:12; Rom. 1:32 | 6:1–11—wronging and defrauding one another |
| rejoices in the truth | finds joy in the truth, in God's way | John 3:21; 1 John 3:18; 2 John 4; 3 John 3–4 | |
| bears all things | endures, withstands, keeps confidential(?) | 9:12; 1 Thess. 3:5 | |
| believes all things | never loses faith (NLT); no limit to its faith (NEB) | 13:13 | |
| hopes all things | is always hopeful (NLT); no limit to its hope (NEB) | 13:13 | |
| endures all things | always perseveres (NIV) | 13:4 | |

## Weapons Piled Up High (13:8–13)

Paul sounds the final note to his rhapsody on love in verse 8: "love never fails" (NIV). It will always be there. We won't hear about love again until verse 13, for Paul hurries to set up a contrast between love and the gifts of the Spirit. If *love* is bound up in God's character and will endure unto eternity, *gifts* have a limited shelf life. The gifts listed in verse 8—prophecy, tongues, and knowledge—are not special cases; they represent all the gifts mentioned so far (12:8–10, 28–30; 13:1–2). And each one is slated for demolition.

> ***Argument by Counterexample***
>
> By stating what love is not, Paul "tips off the alert reader immediately that love is the opposite of the divisive rivalry that he has deplored in Corinth."—Hays, *First Corinthians,* Interpretation, 226.

Prophecy and knowledge, Paul says, "will be abolished" (Greek: *katargeo*). God intends to nullify them when they are no longer necessary. Likewise, tongues will "be stilled" (NIV; Greek: *pauo*). The fact that Paul employs a different verb with tongues—tongues will "be stilled"; prophecy and knowledge will "be abolished"—has generated much interest among those who, like Brother Mel, think tongues are now passé. But Paul is not predicting the early demise of tongues; he is simply avoiding tedious repetition. God gives all three gifts, and God gets to decide when to stop giving.

> Other scriptures affirm the durability of love, too: "Many waters cannot quench love, neither can floods drown it" (Song of Solomon 8:7).

Verses 9–10 are commentary on verse 8. This present age is the age of the Spirit, marked by gifts "suited to the time between the times, when the church must walk by faith" (Hays, 229). No gift is designed to answer every question or fill every gap; "we know only in part, and we prophesy only in part." Even when a gift like prophesy is working precisely as it should, it can provide only a partial revelation, "a real but imperfect glimpse of God's future truth" (Hays, 229).

Ah, but "when the perfect comes," Paul adds in verse 10, "the partial will be done away" (NASV). How should we understand this contrast between the perfect and the partial, between the complete and the incomplete? When exactly does the "perfect" come? This is the kind of expression that fuels late-night debates between folks like Louie and Mel. Those who agree with Mel might argue that the "perfect" refers to the perfection or completion of the canon; when the last New Testament book was finished, charismatic gifts like prophecy and tongues became obsolete. Or perhaps they might claim, with much "throat-clearing" and "anguished looks," that the "perfect" arrived when the church came of age and traded in her childish preoccupation with things miraculous for a mature focus on love and godly leadership. Either way, all parties should "take a closer look" at the context, and especially verse 12.

Verses 11 and 12 contain two analogies—illustrations that Paul hoped would illuminate his meaning. He first considers the difference between a young child and a grown man. It's as if Paul took two snapshots out of his wallet. Here's me, Paul says, as a young lad. As you can see, everything about me—my speech, my thinking, my reasoning—is childish. But now look at me in this shot—I'm all grown up, and all the marks of childhood have vanished. The point is not that children gradually grow up into adults, but rather that these two stages are so radically different. So it is with the people of God. Spiritual gifts rightly belong in this age, but they would be entirely out of place in the age to come.

## Want to Know More?

**About the gift of tongues?** See Frank Stagg, E. Glenn Hinson, and Wayne E. Oates, *Glossolalia: Tongue Speaking in Biblical, Historical, and Psychological Perspective* (Nashville: Abingdon Press, 1967), and Watson E. Mills, *Speaking in Tongues: A Guide to Research on Glossolalia* (Grand Rapids: Wm. B. Eerdmans Publishing Co., 1986).

**About the biblical words for "love"?** See William Barclay, *New Testament Words* (Philadelphia: Westminster Press, 1974), 17–30. For a classic on this topic, see C. S. Lewis, *The Four Loves* (New York: Harcourt Brace, 1960).

Paul's second image is of someone looking in a mirror. Because ancient Corinth was known for manufacturing mirrors out of bronze, this illustration was sure to get their attention. To view someone's reflection is, obviously, to see indirectly; however fine the image, it is not as good as a direct, personal encounter. By analogy, there will come a day when our indirect and incomplete understanding of God will be replaced with a face-to-face encounter. Jacob had a "face-to-face" encounter with God by the ford of the river Jabbok and barely lived to tell about it (Gen. 32:30). And God angrily told Aaron and Miriam that their brother Moses was not just any prophet: "With him I speak face to face—clearly, not in riddles" (Num. 12:8; cf. Ex. 33:11; Deut. 34:10). These awesome encounters between the patriarchs and their Lord give us a hint of what is to come, when all of us will enjoy the presence of God—not just the patriarchs and the apostles, but also the Aarons and the Miriams, the Louies and the Mels. No more painful debates about whether "the Spirit has led" or about what "the Spirit has written in big black letters." Everyone will be able to see it clearly. So the "perfect" of verse 10 can only be the end of the age, the fulfillment of God's resurrection promises and the establishment of God's universal rule. Only then will the need for spiritual gifts disappear.

In the meantime, says verse 13, three things remain—faith, hope, and love. These three

> are the enduring character marks of the Christian life in the present time, in this anomalous interval between the cross and the *parousia.* Faith is the trust that we direct toward the God of Israel, who has kept faith with his covenant promises by putting forward Jesus for our sake and raising him to new life; hope focuses our fervent desire to see a broken world restored by God to its rightful wholeness; . . . and love is the foretaste of our ultimate union with God, graciously given to us now and shared with our brothers and sisters. (Hays, 230–31)

For Paul this triad of virtues encompasses, one way or another, all that it means to be Christian (cf. Rom. 5:1–5; Gal. 5:5–6; 1 Thess. 1:3; 5:8; Eph. 4:2–5; Col. 1:4–5). But among the three, *love* stands out as the greatest because only love will survive into eternity. The long walk of *faith* will be behind us when we finally open our eyes to walk by sight (2 Cor. 5:5–8). And *hope* will dissolve (no doubt, in tears) when we finally encounter the One for whom we have yearned for so long (Rom. 8:22–25). And even those gifts, given to sustain us in the interim, sometimes used rightly and sometimes abused—they will all simply be turned in, like so many weapons piled up high to signal that the war is finally over.

> "When love is entered into, there comes into life a relationship against which the assaults of time are helpless and which transcends death."—Barclay, *The Letters to the Corinthians,* 125.

Whether our struggle to love one another is played out in a home Bible study or a congregational meeting, a mission compound or a construction site, it is well worth reminding each other that love is *the one thing* that connects us with the world to come.

## ? Questions for Reflection

1. The previous unit helped explain the function of the gifts of the Spirit. This unit was about love. What is the relationship between love and the gifts?

2. The term "love" may be used in many ways. I may "love" my job, or a great book, or even chocolate ice cream. How should we define love? What is Paul's definition of love?
3. As noted in this unit, we often hear this passage cited at weddings or with reference to relationships between two individuals. But Paul addressed this letter to a community. How can we apply love practically to a larger body of people? What does it mean to believe-endure-hope all things for a whole group? What if there are competing interests in the group?
4. As Paul is wrapping up in verse 12, he states that "he will know fully, even as he has been fully known." What is Paul speaking about? What will he know fully?

# 1 Corinthians 14:26–40 10

# *All Things Done Decently and in Order*

"Anyone who lies down and sleeps in a session of the congregation shall be punished for thirty days."

"Anyone who bursts into foolish horse laughter is to be punished by reduced rations for thirty days."

"A man who spits into the midst of a session of the congregation is to be punished by reduced rations for thirty days." (Adapted from Wise, 136)

You have to admire those Jewish monks of Paul's day—those sectarian keepers of the Dead Sea Scrolls who lived together out there in the Judean desert. Their little community, in ruins since Roman troops moved through in 70 C.E., perches on a plateau high above the Dead Sea, about thirteen miles east of Jerusalem. Today we call it *Qumran* (pronounced Koom-rón). They may have moved out there in protest, or in self-defense, or because they felt called to establish a "last days" community to prepare for the final cosmic battle. But whatever the reason, they took themselves very seriously. If you wanted to join, you would face two years of probation; once you were in, you pooled your wealth and embraced a highly structured and rigidly hierarchical way of life.

The Qumran community dwelled near the Dead Sea.

The rules listed up above come from a document that apparently governed daily life in the community. When they gathered for Bible study and worship, they wanted to get it right. So they established rules: about falling asleep and laughing and spitting, about leaving the room without permission, and about interruptions during a service. On and on it goes. It would be grossly unfair to say that religion for them was simply a matter of keeping the rules; from what we can tell, they lived a disciplined life together, full of mealtime discussions, Bible reading, secret teachings, sacred rituals, and corporate prayer. But one thing is clear: members of the Qumran community displayed a remarkable zeal for order, hierarchy, and protocol.

It's a long way from that quiet little settlement by the sea to the bustling Christian community in Corinth: from Judea all the way to Achaia; from Biblical Hebrew to common Greek; from desert monastery to inner-city church. It's like moving from the prairies of western Canada to a suburb of Los Angeles. We leave behind the monkish concern for orderly conduct and sober propriety, only to encounter the frenzied charismania of a Christian community coming of age in the shadow of paganism. Which is why Paul must write this section of his letter, and why he must lay down some rules and principles for proper behavior in church. As we watch Paul at work, and as we ponder the constraints he wants to place on Christian worship, it may be worth asking how different things would have been had his commission come, not from the Christians in Jerusalem and Antioch, but from the sectarian community at Qumran.

> "[This] letter . . . shows us a church in the first flush of youth, a completely new group which is trying to get itself organized."—Lucas Grollenberg, *Paul* (Philadelphia: Westminster Press, 1978), 101.

## Sharing the Microphone (14:26–33)

These eight verses allow us to peer back into the past, to see what it must have been like to "go to church" in Paul's day. Or rather they provide a glimpse of how Paul's model church would function. Corinthian readers would immediately recognize how far their disorderly and self-centered behavior fell short of this ideal. The vivid picture Paul sketches is

> of a free-flowing community gathering under the guidance of the Holy Spirit in which "each one" contributes something to the mix.

> Clearly there was no fixed order of service, no printed bulletin for the worshipers! Nor—more remarkably—is anything said of a leader to preside over the meeting. Apparently Paul expects all the members to follow the promptings of the Spirit, taking turns in offering their gifts for the benefit of the assembly, deferring to one another (vv. 29–30) and learning from one another. (Hays, 241)

Paul's list of ways to contribute to the assembly (v. 26) is no more comprehensive than his earlier catalogues of spiritual gifts (12:8–10, 28–30; 13:1–2; 14:6). "Each one" (not "everyone," as in NIV) could do something: perhaps offer a psalm, deliver a teaching, present a revelation, speak in a tongue, or provide an interpretation. We encountered "singing" back in verse 15 in the context of tongues. Apparently some tongues were expressed melodically; on other occasions the entire congregation sang to one another and "to the Lord" (Eph. 5:19; cf. Col. 3:16). Verse 26 may envision someone suggesting a psalm or perhaps singing a solo. Some songs were no doubt familiar to all, whereas others were composed on the spot. Either way, music played a part in Christian worship from the very beginning (cf. Matt. 26:30; Mark 14:26). "Teaching" may refer to Spirit-inspired instruction, or to careful exposition of scripture, or both (cf. 14:6, 19; 12:28–29; Eph. 4:11; Acts 2:42).

> "The really notable thing about an early Church service must have been that almost everyone came feeling . . . both the privilege and the obligation of contributing something to it."—Barclay, *The Letters to the Corinthians,* 134.

What would happen if we were to take more seriously Paul's emphasis on each member's unique contribution? Would we be less concerned that our services adhere tightly to the "script," and more open to follow the Spirit's leading? Would we be more ready to encourage even the young and the timid to present their gifts, however unadorned or underdeveloped? Perhaps we would yearn, with Philip Jacob Spener, the German pastor of the seventeenth century, for a church that is less dependent upon professionals to do the work of edification:

> We preachers cannot instruct the people from our pulpits as much as is needful unless other persons in the congregation, who by God's grace have a superior knowledge of Christianity, take the pains . . . to work with and under us to correct and reform as much in their neighbors as they are able according to the measure of their gifts and their simplicity. (Spener, 13)

Of course, whenever we encourage lay ministry we take risks. Not everyone will show discernment. Some will lack polish. Others won't want to share the microphone. So Paul adds verses 27–33 to make sure that spontaneity doesn't translate into chaos. Verses 27–28 focus on speaking in tongues: two or three at a time, Paul says, not in competition but taking turns, and with at least one interpreter. Paul's language here ("only two or at most three") shows he is not so much chiseling a new law code as he is offering practical advice intended to keep tongues (or any other gift) in their place. The community gathers not to give individuals a chance to strut their spiritual stuff, but to give opportunity for everyone to be built up by one another (cf. 14:3, 4, 5, 12, 17).

The important principle in verse 28 relates to self-control. Those who speak out in tongues should know, or should pause to find out, if there is someone present to interpret. If not, they should sit back down and "speak to themselves and to God." As Hays remarks:

> These directives presume that the gift is in some sense under the speaker's control. . . . Paul does not think of the gift of tongues as an overpowering emotional experience in which the speaker is possessed by the Spirit in some sort of ecstatic trance. (Hays, 241–42)

Verses 29–33 apply similar standards to prophecy: "two or three prophets" are plenty at any one time. Paul would be happy to see all of them prophesy at one point or another (cf. 14:5, 24, 31), but there would be little gained from an unceasing string of messages unless the community regularly paused to assess their significance. So, after you've heard from several prophets, "let the others weigh what is said" (NRSV). The "others" here are not the other prophets, as though the task fell to an elite cohort, but simply the rest of the congregation. Prophecies, once offered, are in the public domain. They are not self-interpreting; they are not independently authoritative; they are not automatically genuine. If someone believes he or she has received a message from the Lord for the congregation, he or she must share it in humility, recognizing that the assembly as a whole must discern whether it is authentic, what it means, and how the church should respond (cf. 1 Thess. 5:19–22).

Verses 30–31 place further restrictions on prophetic speech. Apparently some prophets would go on speaking for some time, for Paul says, "If a revelation is made to someone else sitting nearby, let the first person be silent" (NRSV). As with tongues, there is no corporate advantage if several prophesy at the same time or if one individual is allowed to dominate the assembly.

Verses 32 and 33 enfold all of these very practical guidelines in two deeply theological principles:

1. "*The spirits of the prophets are subject to the prophets*" (*v. 32*). Christian prophets cannot rightly claim to be "possessed" or "controlled" by their gift. It works the other way around. Evidently, some in Corinth would have challenged Paul on this point.
2. "*God is a God not of disorder but of peace*" (*v. 33*). Christians who gather together should behave like the God they worship. So there should be "neither stiff formality nor undisciplined frenzy" but rather something "more like a complex but graceful dance, or a beautiful anthem sung in counterpoint" (Hays, 243).

Note that the converse of "disorder" is not "order," for God does not evaluate the quality of Christian worship in terms of promptness and predictability. Rarely does the Holy Spirit show up on time. Rather, if we are to reflect the character of our God, we should conduct ourselves in "peace" toward one another. We might well ask in passing how our corporate worship might display other divine attributes. How do our gatherings manifest the *holiness* of God? Or what about God's *joyfulness?* Is our worship *truthful?* Do we behave *graciously* toward one another? The fact that Paul could not charge too many contemporary churches with raucous disorder does not guarantee that our worship does any better at reflecting God's character.

How should we understand the final clause of verse 33? It could function as the beginning of the next paragraph: "As in all the churches of the saints, women should be silent in the churches" (NRSV; cf. NIV, NEB, NJB). But the awkward repetition of "in the churches" (hard to see in the NIV) makes this unlikely. It probably belongs as the conclusion of this section: God wants peace to mark the worship of believers not just in Corinth but everywhere (cf. NASV, KJV, NLT).

## Young Birds Before They Can Fly (14:34–36)

This is one of those knotty passages that tend to provoke strong reactions, for obvious reasons. On the face of it, Paul appears to be requiring *all* women to forswear *all* speaking during *every* gathering of the assembly. Our first instinct may be to repudiate these verses outright or at least to scurry rapidly over such difficult terrain, but if Paul has shown himself trustworthy on other points, perhaps he deserves our respectful attention here as well. Off we go, then, on a brief tour of four (of the many) ways these words have been understood. Although this author finds the fourth approach most persuasive, we will leave it to the reader to "weigh what is said."

1. *Paul's editor shows his hand.* Some have argued that verses 34–35 were not originally part of Paul's letter. Rather, they were inserted deliberately by an ancient scribe who seized a chance to restrict the activities of women (perhaps in the face of a rising feminist movement or under the influence of 1 Tim. 2:11–12). Paul is writing about *order* in church and about the need for *silence* (14:28, 30); what better place to insert remarks about the *orderly silence* of women? The case for this view is surprisingly strong: (1) Only a few chapters back (11:5, 13) Paul was implicitly encouraging women to pray and prophesy publicly (provided their heads were suitably attired). How then can Paul ask for silence here? (2) A handful of Greek and Latin manuscripts of the New Testament relocate verses 34–35 to the end of the chapter, suggesting there was some dispute over where (or whether?) they rightly belong. (3) Paul's argument reads much more smoothly if verse 36 follows directly after verse 33. (4) Several phrases seem odd. Why should women be silent "in the churches" (plural) if this letter was written to *the* church at Corinth (1:1)? And where in the Old Testament does "the law" promote the silence of women? Finally, (5) we know women contributed significantly to the life of Paul's churches (e.g., Acts 18:18–26; Rom. 16:1–4, 7; Phil. 4:2–3; cf. Acts 2:17–18). For those who take this approach, the difficulty these verses present largely disappears.

2. *Women are excluded from positions of authority.* As we have seen, the previous paragraph (14:29–32) envisions several prophets sharing their oracles with the larger community, which was expected to sift the wheat from the chaff—to separate divine insights from merely human opinion (v. 29). In light of chapter 11 (v. 5), we must assume that women were active as prophets in the church. Here in chapter 14, however, Paul calls for their silence during the public evaluation of prophetic oracles. Advocates of this view contend that, for Paul, "weighing" prophecy carried more authoritative "weight" than did prophecy itself. So although Paul readily acknowledged women prophets, he would not let them

occupy positions of authority in the church (cf. 1 Tim. 2:11–15). Church leadership today should likewise be limited to men.

3. *Charismatic women are losing control.* According to a third view, Paul called for women's silence, in the context of his restrictions on tongues and prophecy, because he believed their use of these gifts had gotten out of hand. Perhaps there had been outbursts of ecstatic frenzy, not unlike the ravings displayed in the worship of Dionysus (or Bacchus) at Rome. Pagan practices were infiltrating the church (cf. 6:1; 8:10; 11:20–22). So today, women and men who exercise their gifts appropriately should be free to participate fully in the assembly. Several problems make this view less likely, however. Not only women but also men were known for outrageous behavior in the cults of the day. Moreover, the language of verse 35 seems to imply that women were blurting out pointed questions rather than ecstatic gibberish.

## Want to Know More?

**About Qumran?** See Klaus Berger, *The Truth under Lock and Key? Jesus and the Dead Sea Scrolls* (Louisville, Ky.: Westminster John Knox Press, 1995).

**About Paul and the role of women?** See Roetzel, *The Letters of Paul,* 182–90; Judith M. Gundry-Volf, "Paul on Women and Gender: A Comparison with Early Jewish Views," in *The Road from Damascus: The Impact of Paul's Conversion on His Life, Thought, and Ministry,* ed. Richard N. Longnecker (Grand Rapids: Wm. B. Eerdmans Publishing Co., 1997), 184–212; and Hawthorne, Martin, and Reid, *Dictionary of Paul and His Letters,* 583–592.

4. *Poorly educated women are interrupting the service.* A fourth view seeks to explain the puzzling prohibition of verse 34 ("women should be silent") in terms of the details of verse 35. So Paul is not forbidding *all* speaking but rather the *public asking of questions.* "If," says Paul, "there is anything they desire to learn," the women should "ask their own husbands at home." In other words, Paul commends private times of discussion and learning, but disallows public interruptions during church assemblies. His vision was for an open and dynamic gathering of believers (14:26–33), but not for pandemonium.

Paul was not the only one to speak out against distracting interruptions during public meetings. Plutarch, a prolific writer and popular lecturer who grew up not far from Corinth during Paul's ministry, wrote an entire essay on the virtue of listening and another on the vice of talkativeness. It is "scandalous," writes Plutarch, "to speak while being spoken to." How much better the one "who has acquired the ability to listen in a self-controlled and respectful fashion" (*On Listening* 4 [39C]). Furthermore, "people who try to divert the speaker on to other topics and interrupt with questions and queries are disagreeable nuisances" (10 [42F]). Paul might have chuckled with approval had he lived to read Plutarch's protest against lazy people who

> bother the speaker . . . by asking the same questions over and over again—they remind one of young birds before they can fly, with their mouths constantly opened towards someone else's mouth, for whom acceptable fare is only what is ready-made and pre-processed by others. (18 [48A])

> "It would certainly be very wrong to take these words out of their context and make them a universal rule for the Church."—Barclay, *The Letters to the Corinthians,* 136.

In Paul's Corinth, particularly among the working classes (which were well represented in the church; cf. 1:26), education would be much more common among men than among women. Apparently several of these unlearned women had crossed a line and were displaying disruptive behavior many would have considered shameful or disgraceful. But Paul's remedy was not intended to demean women.

> To the contrary, Paul is advocating the most progressive view of his day: despite the possibility that she is less educated than himself, the husband should recognize his wife's intellectual capability and therefore make himself responsible for her education, so they can discuss intellectual issues together. (Keener, 84).

In this view, Paul's advice would doubtless sound quite different had he faced a group of particularly unruly men or had more of the women enjoyed the benefits of education. But surely the task of identifying shameful patterns of behavior in the church remains as important today as ever.

Although verse 36 is something of a puzzle, it makes good sense if Paul is resuming the thought he began in verse 33: God's people in churches everywhere, including Corinth, should worship God in peace, not in disorder (v. 33); that is, unless you Corinthians are the sole originators or the sole recipients of God's word (v. 36). In that case, you should feel free to set your own rules. Otherwise, smarten up! As Gordon Fee observes, "Paul is urging them not only to conform to the character of God, but also to get in step with the rest of his church" (Fee, 698).

## Playing the Trump Card (14:37–40)

Paul plays his trump card in verses 37–38. He has argued the need for diversity in the church (chap. 12), he has sung the praises of love (chap. 13), and he has spelled out the principle of edification (chap. 14). No doubt after all this Paul is hopeful many of his readers will be persuaded to change their ways. But if they aren't, he briskly reminds them that "what I am writing to you is a command of the Lord" (v. 37, NRSV). Paul is an apostle, a representative *of* the Lord who speaks *for* the Lord (1:1; 4:14–21; 9:1–2; 11:1; 12:28). So "anyone who defies these teachings by refusing to recognize Paul's authority in this matter will suffer the consequences" (Hays, 244).

The sober warning of verse 38 may be lost on some English readers. Paul is not asking the congregation to snub any who resist Paul's authority, as the NRSV might imply: "anyone who does not recognize this is not to be recognized." More likely, the point is that "failure to recognize the Spirit in Paul's letter will lead to that person's failure to be 'recognized' by God" (Fee, 712; cf. NEB). To reject God's messenger is to forfeit God's salvation.

A final note sounds in verses 39–40: prophecy, hopefully; tongues, possibly; self-control, absolutely. Paul yearns for them to experience every good gift the Spirit has to offer (cf. 14:5, 31). He celebrates diversity, plurality, spontaneity, flexibility, and liberty. Nevertheless, Paul concludes, "all things should be done decently and in order" (NRSV). Rules and restrictions must not "quench the Spirit" (1 Thess. 5:19); they must encourage those who receive God's grace-gifts also to reflect God's gracious character.

> "If, however, God is a God of peace, the Corinthians should learn to be at peace with one another and to express that peace in a style of worship that emphasizes concord and complementarity."—Hays, *First Corinthians*, Interpretation, 243.

## Questions for Reflection

1. Paul is trying to correct some improper practices and give rules for orderly worship. How would you describe your church's worship style? Does it follow a "tight script" or is it more spontaneous? What impact might Paul's words here have on the worship at your church?

2. The writer of this study offers four explanations for the verses that speak about the silence of women in church (vv. 34–35). Which of the four do you agree with, or would you suggest another? Why?
3. Paul states in verse 31 that all can prophesy. Do you think Paul is granting permission for all to try it out for a "test ride," or is Paul acknowledging that God may give the gift to all? What are some reasons to support your position?
4. In Hays' commentary, he encourages readers to take to heart the words of this passage, that it "beckons us to a window through which we glimpse a strange new world of spiritual power" (Hays, 251). What is that "new world" of which Hays speaks?

# Bibliography


Bettenson, Henry. *Documents of the Christian Church.* New York: Oxford University Press, 1963.

Broneer, Oscar. "The Apostle Paul and the Isthmian Games." *Biblical Archaeologist* 25 (1962): 2–31.

Capon, Robert Farrar. *The Romance of the Word: One Man's Love Affair with Theology.* Grand Rapids: Wm. B. Eerdmans Publishing Co., 1995.

Chesterton, G. K. *Orthodoxy: The Romance of Faith.* New York: Dodd, Mead & Co., 1908; reprint, Garden City, N.Y.: Doubleday & Co., 1959.

Colson, Charles. *The Body: Being Light in Darkness.* Dallas, Tex.: Word, 1992.

Fee, Gordon D. *The First Epistle to the Corinthians.* New International Commentary on the New Testament. Grand Rapids: Wm. B. Eerdmans Publishing Co., 1987.

Fischer, John. *Real Christians Don't Dance.* Minneapolis: Bethany House, 1988.

Grahame, Kenneth. *The Wind in the Willows.* New York: Charles Scribner's Sons, 1908; reprint, 1959.

Hays, Richard B. *First Corinthians.* Interpretation: A Bible Commentary for Teaching and Preaching. Louisville, Ky.: John Knox Press, 1997.

Heaven's Gate. Website: http://www.heavensgatetoo.com.

Huxley, Aldous. *Brave New World.* 1932; reprint, New York: Harper & Row, 1969.

Johnson, Luke. *The Writings of the New Testament: An Interpretation.* Philadelphia: Fortress Press, 1986.

Jordan, Clarence. *The Cotton Patch Version of Paul's Epistles.* New York: Association Press, 1968.

Keener, Craig. S. *Paul, Women and Wives.* Peabody, Mass.: Hendrickson, 1992.

Keillor, Garrison. *Lake Wobegon Days.* New York: Viking Penguin Books, 1985.

———. *Leaving Home: A Collection of Lake Wobegon Stories.* New York: Viking Penguin Books, 1987.

Lewis, C. S. *The Great Divorce.* New York: Macmillan Co., 1946.

———. *The Screwtape Letters.* New York: Macmillan Co., 1961.

Malherbe, Abraham J. *Moral Exhortation: A Greco-Roman Sourcebook.* Philadelphia: Westminster Press, 1986.

Neuhaus, Richard John. *Freedom for Ministry.* Rev. ed. Grand Rapids: Wm. B. Eerdmans Publishing Co., 1992.

Plutarch. *Essays.* Translated by R. Waterfield. New York: Penguin Books, 1992.

Pyle, Howard. *The Story of King Arthur and His Knights.* New York: Grosset & Dunlap, 1965.

Russell, Bertrand. *Why I Am Not a Christian.* New York: Simon & Schuster, 1957.

Sophocles. *Oedipus Rex.*

Spener, Philip Jacob. *Pia Desideria.* 1675. Translated by T. G. Tappert. Philadelphia: Fortress Press, 1964.

Steinbeck, John. *The Pearl.* New York: Viking Press, 1947.

Tolkien, J. R. R. *The Lord of the Rings.* New York: Ballantine Books, 1965.

Wiesel, Elie. *Night.* London: MacGibbon & Kee, 1960.

Willard, Dallas. *The Spirit of the Disciplines.* San Francisco: Harper & Row, 1988.

Wise, M., M. Abegg, Jr., and E. Cook. *The Dead Sea Scrolls: A New Translation.* San Francisco: Harper, 1996.

Wright, N. T. *What Saint Paul Really Said: Was Paul of Tarsus the Real Founder of Christianity?* Grand Rapids: Wm. B. Eerdmans Publishing Co., 1997.

# Interpretation Bible Studies Leader's Guide

Interpretation Bible Studies (IBS), for adults and older youth, are flexible, attractive, easy-to-use, and filled with solid information about the Bible. IBS helps Christians discover the guidance and power of the scriptures for living today. Perhaps you are leading a church school class, a midweek Bible study group, or a youth group meeting, or simply using this in your own personal study. Whatever the setting may be, we hope you find this *Leader's Guide* helpful. Since every context and group is different, this *Leader's Guide* does not presume to tell you how to structure Bible study for your situation. Instead, the *Leader's Guide* seeks to offer choices—a number of helpful suggestions for leading a successful Bible study using IBS.

"The church that no longer hears the essential message of the Scriptures soon ceases to understand what it is for and is open to be captured by the dominant religious philosophy of the moment." —James D. Smart, *The Strange Silence of the Bible in the Church: A Study in Hermeneutics* (Philadelphia: Westminster Press, 1970), 10.

## How Should I Teach IBS?

### 1. Explore the Format

There is a wealth of information in IBS, perhaps more than you can use in one session. In this case, more is better. IBS has been designed to give you a well-stocked buffet of content and teachable insights. Pick and choose what suits your group's needs. Perhaps you will want to split units into two or more sessions, or combine units into a single session. Perhaps you will decide to use only a portion of a unit and then move on to the next unit. *There is not a structured theme or teaching focus to each unit that must be followed for IBS to be used.* Rather, IBS offers the flexibility to adjust to whatever suits your context.

> "The more we bring to the Bible, the more we get from the Bible."—William Barclay, *A Beginner's Guide to the New Testament* (Louisville, Ky.: Westminster John Knox Press, 1995), vii.

A recent survey of both professional and volunteer church educators revealed that their number one concern was that Bible study materials be teacher-friendly. IBS is indeed teacher-friendly in two important ways. First, since IBS provides abundant content and a flexible design, teachers can shape the lessons creatively, responding to the needs of the group and employing a wide variety of teaching methods. Second, those who wish more specific suggestions for planning the sessions can find them at the Geneva Press web site on the Internet (**www.wjkbooks.com**). Click the "Downloads" button to access teaching suggestions for each IBS unit as well as helpful quotations, selections from Bible dictionaries and encyclopedias, and other teaching helps.

IBS is not only teacher-friendly, it is also discussion-friendly. Given the opportunity, most adults and young people relish the chance to talk about the kind of issues raised in IBS. The secret, then, is to determine what works with your group, what will get them to talk. Several good methods for stimulating discussion are presented in this *Leader's Guide*, and once you learn your group, you can apply one of these methods and get the group discussing the Bible and its relevance in their lives.

The format of every IBS unit consists of several features:

**a. Body of the Unit.** This is the main content, consisting of interesting and informative commentary on the passage and scholarly insight into the biblical text and its significance for Christians today.

**b. Sidebars.** These are boxes that appear scattered throughout the body of the unit, with maps, photos, quotations, and intriguing ideas. Some sidebars can be identified quickly by a symbol, or icon, that helps the reader know what type of information can be found in that sidebar. There are icons for illustrations, key terms, pertinent quotes, and more.

**c. Want to Know More?** Each unit includes a "Want to Know More?" section that guides learners who wish to dig deeper and consult other resources. If your church library does not have the resources mentioned, you can look up the information in other standard Bible dictionaries, encyclopedias, and handbooks, or you can find much of this information at the Geneva Press Web site (see last page of this Guide).

**d. Questions for Reflection.** The unit ends with questions to help the learners think more deeply about the biblical passage and its pertinence for today. These questions are provided as examples only, and teachers are encouraged both to develop their own list of questions and to gather questions from the group. These discussion questions do not usually have specific "correct" answers. Again, the flexibility of IBS allows you to use these questions at the end of the group time, at the beginning, interspersed throughout, or not at all.

"The trick is to make the Bible our book." —Duncan S. Ferguson, *Bible Basics: Mastering the Content of the Bible* (Louisville, Ky.: Westminster John Knox Press, 1995), 3.

## 2. Select a Teaching Method

Here are ten suggestions. The format of IBS allows you to choose what direction you will take as you plan to teach. Only you will know how your lesson should best be designed for your group. Some adult groups prefer the lecture method, while others prefer a high level of free-ranging discussion. Many youth groups like interaction, activity, the use of music, and the chance to talk about their own experiences and feelings. Here is a list of a few possible approaches. Let your own creativity add to the list!

**a. Let's Talk about What We've Learned.** In this approach, all group members are requested to read the scripture passage and the IBS unit before the group meets. Ask the group members to make notes about the main issues, concerns, and questions they see in the passage. When the group meets, these notes are collected, shared, and discussed. This method depends, of course, on the group's willingness to do some "homework."

**b. What Do We Want and Need to Know?** This approach begins by having the whole group read the scripture passage together. Then, drawing from your study of the IBS, you, as the teacher, write on a board or flip chart two lists:

(1) Things we should know to better understand this passage (content information related to the passage, for example, historical insights about political contexts, geographical landmarks, economic nuances, etc.), and

(2) Four or five "important issues we should talk about regarding this passage" (with implications for today—how the issues in the biblical context continue into today, for example, issues of idolatry or fear).

Allow the group to add to either list, if they wish, and use the lists to lead into a time of learning, reflection, and discussion. This approach is suitable for those settings where there is little or no advanced preparation by the students.

"Although small groups can meet for many purposes and draw upon many different resources, the one resource which has shaped the life of the Church more than any other throughout its long history has been the Bible." —Roberta Hestenes, *Using the Bible in Groups* (Philadelphia: Westminster Press, 1983), 14.

**c. Hunting and Gathering.** Start the unit by having the group read the scripture passage together. Then divide the group into smaller clusters (perhaps having as few as one person), each with a different assignment. Some clusters can discuss one or more of the "Questions for Reflection." Others can look up key terms or people in a Bible dictionary or track down other biblical references found in the body of the unit. After the small clusters have had time to complete their tasks, gather the entire group again and lead them through the study material, allowing each cluster to contribute what it learned.

**d. From Question Mark to Exclamation Point.** This approach begins with contemporary questions and then moves to the biblical content as a response to those questions. One way to do this is for you to ask the group, at the beginning of the class, a rephrased version of one or more of the "Questions for Reflection" at the end of the study unit. For example, one of the questions at the end of the unit on Exodus 3:1–4:17 in the IBS *Exodus* volume reads,

> Moses raised four protests, or objections, to God's call. Contemporary people also raise objections to God's call. In what ways are these similar to Moses' protests? In what ways are they different?

This question assumes familiarity with the biblical passage about Moses, so the question would not work well before the group has explored the passage. However, try rephrasing this question as an opening exercise; for example:

> Here is a thought experiment: Let's assume that God, who called people in the Bible to do daring and risky things, still calls people today to tasks of faith and courage. In the Bible, God called Moses from a burning bush and called Isaiah in a moment of ecstatic worship in the Temple. How do you think God's call is experienced by people today? Where do you see evidence of people saying "yes" to God's call? When people say "no" or raise an objection to God's call, what reasons do they give (to themselves, to God)?

Posing this or a similar question at the beginning will generate discussion and raise important issues, and then it can lead the group into an exploration of the biblical passage as a resource for thinking even more deeply about these questions.

**e. Let's Go to the Library**. From your church library, your pastor's library, or other sources, gather several good commentaries on the book of the Bible you are studying. Among the trustworthy commentaries are those in the Interpretation series (John Knox Press) and the Westminster Bible Companion series (Westminster John Knox Press). Divide your group into smaller clusters and give one commentary to each cluster (one or more of the clusters can be given the IBS volume instead of a full-length commentary). Ask each cluster to read the biblical passage you are studying and then to read the section of the commentary that covers that passage (if your group is large, you may want to make photocopies of the commentary material with proper permission, of course). The task of each cluster is to name the two or three most important insights they discover about the biblical passage by reading and talking together about the commentary material. When you reassemble the larger group to share these insights, your group will gain not only a variety of insights about the passage but also a sense that differing views of the same text are par for the course in biblical interpretation.

**f. Working Creatively Together**. Begin with a creative group task, tied to the main thrust of the study. For example, if the study is on the Ten Commandments, a parable, or a psalm, have the group rewrite the Ten Commandments, the parable, or the psalm in contemporary language. If the passage is an epistle, have the group write a letter to their own congregation. Or if the study is a narrative, have the group role-play the characters in the story or write a page describing the story from the point of view of one of the characters. After completion of the task, read and discuss the biblical passage, asking for interpretations and applications from the group and tying in IBS material as it fits the flow of the discussion.

**g. Singing Our Faith.** Begin the session by singing (or reading) together a hymn that alludes to the biblical passage being studied (or to the theological themes in the passage). Most hymnals have an index of scriptural allusions. For example, if you are studying the unit from the IBS volume on Psalm 121, you can sing "I to the Hills Will Lift My Eyes," "Sing Praise to God, Who Reigns Above," or another hymn based on Psalm 121. Let the group reflect on the thoughts and feelings evoked by the hymn, then move to the biblical passage, allowing the biblical text and the IBS material to underscore, clarify, refine, and deepen the discussion stimulated by the hymn. If you are ambitious, you may ask the group to write a new hymn at the end of the study! (Many hymnals have indexes in the back or companion volumes that help the user match hymns to scripture passages or topics.)

**h. Fill in the Blanks.** In order to help the learners focus on the content of the biblical passage, at the beginning of the session ask each member of the group to read the biblical passage and fill out a brief questionnaire about the details of the passage (provide a copy for each learner or write the questions on the board). For example, if you are studying the unit in the IBS *Matthew* volume on Matthew 22:1–14, the questionnaire could include questions such as the following:

—In this story, Jesus compares the kingdom of heaven to what?
—List the various responses of those who were invited to the king's banquet but who did not come.
—When his invitation was rejected, how did the king feel? What did the king do?
—In the second part of the story, when the king saw a man at the banquet without a wedding garment, what did the king say? What did the man say? What did the king do?
—What is the saying found at the end of this story?

Gather the group's responses to the questions and perhaps encourage discussion. Then lead the group through the IBS material helping the learners to understand the meanings of these details and the significance of the passage for today. Feeling creative? Instead of a fill-in-the blanks questionnaire, create a crossword puzzle from names and words in the biblical passage.

**i. Get the Picture.** In this approach, stimulate group discussion by incorporating a painting, photograph, or other visual object into the lesson. You can begin by having the group examine and comment on this visual or you can introduce the visual later in the lesson—it depends on the object used. If, for example, you are studying the unit Exodus 3:1–4:17 in the IBS *Exodus* volume, you may want to view Paul Koli's very colorful painting *The Burning Bush.* Two sources for this painting are *The Bible Through Asian Eyes,* edited by Masao Takenaka and Ron O'Grady (National City, Calif.: Pace Publishing Co., 1991), and *Imaging the Word: An Arts and Lectionary Resource,* vol. 3, edited by Susan A. Blain (Cleveland: United Church Press, 1996).

**j. Now Hear This.** Especially if your class is large, you may want to use the lecture method. As the teacher, you prepare a presentation on the biblical passage, using as many resources as you have available plus your own experience, but following the content of the IBS unit as a guide. You can make the lecture even more lively by asking the learners at various points along the way to refer to the visuals and quotes found in the "sidebars." A place can be made for questions (like the ones at the end of the unit)—either at the close of the lecture or at strategic points along the way.

> "It is . . . important to call a Bible study group back to what the text being discussed actually says, especially when an individual has gotten off on some tangent." —Richard Robert Osmer, *Teaching for Faith: A Guide for Teachers of Adult Classes* (Louisville, Ky.: Westminster John Knox Press, 1992), 71.

### 3. Keep These Teaching Tips in Mind

There are no surefire guarantees for a teaching success. However, the following suggestions can increase the chances for a successful study:

**a. Always Know Where the Group Is Headed.** Take ample time beforehand to prepare the material. Know the main points of the study, and know the destination. Be flexible, and encourage discussion, but don't lose sight of where you are headed.

**b. Ask Good Questions; Don't Be Afraid of Silence.** Ideally, a discussion blossoms spontaneously from the reading of the scripture. But more often than not, a discussion must be drawn from the group members by a series of well-chosen questions. After asking each question, give the group members time to answer. Let them think, and don't be threatened by a season of silence. Don't feel that every question must have an answer, and that as leader, you must supply every answer. Facilitate discussion by getting the group members to cooperate with each other. Sometimes, the original question can be restated. Sometimes it is helpful to ask a follow-up question like "What makes this a hard question to answer?"

Ask questions that encourage explanatory answers. Try to avoid questions that can be answered simply "Yes" or "No." Rather than asking, "Do you think Moses was frightened by the burning bush?" ask, "What do you think Moses was feeling and experiencing as he stood before the burning bush?" If group members answer with just one word, ask a follow-up question like "Why do you think this is so?" Ask questions about their feelings and opinions, mixed within questions about facts or details. Repeat their responses or restate their response to reinforce their contributions to the group.

> "Studies of learning reveal that while people remember approximately 10% of what they hear, they remember up to 90% of what they say. Therefore, to increase the amount of learning that occurs, increase the amount of talking about the Bible which each member does."—Roberta Hestenes, *Using the Bible in Groups* (Philadelphia: Westminster Press, 1983), 17.

Most studies can generate discussion by asking open-ended questions. Depending on the group, several types of questions can work. Some groups will respond well to content questions that can be answered from reading the IBS comments or the biblical passage. Others will respond well to questions about feelings or thoughts. Still others will respond to questions that challenge them to new thoughts or that may not have exact answers. Be sensitive to the group's dynamic in choosing questions.

Some suggested questions are: What is the point of the passage? Who are the main characters? Where is the tension in the story? Why does it say (this)____________, and not (that) ____________? What raises questions for you? What terms need defining? What are the new ideas? What doesn't make sense? What bothers or troubles you about this passage? What keeps you from living the truth of this passage?

**c. Don't Settle for the Ordinary.** There is nothing like a surprise. Think of special or unique ways to present the ideas of the study. Upset the applecart of the ordinary. Even though the passage may be familiar, look for ways to introduce suspense. Remember that a little mystery can capture the imagination. Change your routine.

Along with the element of surprise, humor can open up a discussion. Don't be afraid to laugh. A well-chosen joke or cartoon may present the central theme in a way that a lecture would have stymied.

Sometimes a passage is too familiar. No one speaks up because everyone feels that all that could be said has been said. Choose an unfamiliar translation from which to read, or if the passage is from a Gospel, compare the story across two or more Gospels and note differences. It is amazing what insights can be drawn from seeing something strange in what was thought to be familiar.

**d. Feel free to Supplement the IBS Resources with Other Material.** Consult other commentaries to resources. Tie in current events with the lesson. Scour newspapers or magazines for stories that touch on the issues of the study. Sometimes the lyrics of a song, or a section of prose from a well-written novel will be just the right seasoning for the study.

**e. And Don't Forget to Check the Web.** Check out our site on the World Wide Web (www.wjkbooks.com). Click the "Downloads" button to access teaching suggestions. Several possibilities for applying the teaching methods suggested above for individual IBS units will be available. Feel free to download this material.

"The Bible is literature, but it is much more than literature. It is the holy book of Jews and Christians, who find there a manifestation of God's presence."—Kathleen Norris, *The Psalms* (New York: Riverhead Books, 1997), xxii.

**f. Stay Close to the Biblical Text.** Don't forget that the goal is to learn the Bible. Return to the text again and again. Avoid making the mistake of reading the passage only at the beginning of the study, and then wandering away to comments on top of comments from that point on. Trust in the power and presence of the Holy Spirit to use the truths of the passage to work within the lives of the study participants.

## What If Am Using IBS in Personal Bible Study?

If you are using IBS in your personal Bible study, you can experiment and explore a variety of ways. You may choose to read straight through the study without giving any attention to the sidebars or other features. Or you may find yourself interested in a question or unfamiliar with a key term, and you can allow the sidebars "Want to Know More?" and "Questions for Reflection" to lead you into deeper learning on these issues. Perhaps you will want to have a few commentaries or a Bible dictionary available to pursue what interests you. As was suggested in one of the teaching methods above, you may want to begin with the questions at the end, and then read the Bible passage followed by the IBS material. Trust the IBS resources to provide good and helpful information, and then follow your interests!

## Want to Know More?

**About leading Bible study groups?** See Roberta Hestenes, *Using the Bible in Groups* (Philadelphia: Westminster Press, 1983).

**About basic Bible content?** See Duncan S. Ferguson, *Bible Basics: Mastering the Content of the Bible* (Louisville, Ky.: Westminster John Knox Press, 1995); William M. Ramsay, *The Westminster Guide to the Books of the Bible* (Louisville, Ky.: Westminster John Knox Press, 1994).

**About the development of the Bible?** See John Barton, *How the Bible Came to Be* (Louisville, Ky.: Westminster John Knox Press, 1997).

**About the meaning of difficult terms?** See Donald K. McKim, *Westminster Dictionary of Theological Terms* (Louisville, Ky.: Westminster John Knox Press, 1996); Paul J. Achtemeier, *Harper's Bible Dictionary* (San Francisco: Harper & Row, 1985).

**For teaching suggestions for IBS, click the "Downloads" button at www.wjkbooks.com**